WHO WAS JESUS?

Also by N. T. Wright and published by SPCK

The Crown and the Fire
The New Testament and the People of God
Following Jesus
Jesus and the Victory of God
For All God's Worth
The Lord and His Prayer

Who Was Jesus?

N T Wright

First published in Great Britain in 1992

Society for Promoting Christian Knowledge
36 Causton Street
London SW1P 4ST

British Library Cataloguing-in-Publication Data
A catalogue record for this book is available from the British Library.

ISBN-13: 978–0–281–05741–2
ISBN-10: 0–281–05741–9

3 5 7 9 10 8 6 4 2

Typeset by Tom Wright, Oxford, using *Nota Bene* software
First printed in Great Britain by Biddles Ltd, Guildford and King's Lynn
Reprinted in Great Britain by Bookmarque Ltd, Croydon, Surrey

Contents

Preface vii

1. The Portraits and the Puzzles 1

2. Barbara Thiering: Jesus in Code 19

3. A. N. Wilson: A Moderately Pale Galilean 37

4. John Spong: The Bishop and the Birth 65

5. Jesus Revisited 93

Notes 104

For the Chapel Community at Worcester College, Oxford

Preface

In the late summer of 1992, the news media were flooded with stories about Jesus. Or rather, to be exact, stories about stories about Jesus. Amidst a storm of publicity, three books in particular stood out.

The first to hit the shelves, by a short head, was by the Australian scholar Barbara Thiering. Her *Jesus the Man: A New Interpretation from the Dead Sea Scrolls* claimed to be able to read between the lines of the New Testament and to discover there a quite startling picture of Jesus. In particular, she suggested that Jesus had been married, had fathered three children, and had then divorced and married again.

Shortly afterwards, the British journalist and novelist A. N. Wilson published his book, simply entitled *Jesus*. It was accompanied by the media equivalent of a 21-gun salute: articles and reviews in every British paper, interviews on several chat shows, and a television documentary. This book follows Wilson's recent much-publicized rejection of religion in general and of Christianity in particular.

The third similar book was by the well-known Bishop of Newark, New Jersey. John Spong has often hit the headlines through his outspoken support for radical causes. This time, in *Born of a Woman*, he claimed that the doctrine of the Virgin Birth had been responsible for a great deal of oppression of women, and he set out to put the record straight.

For some reason, this 'interest' in Jesus has even reached the level of farce. The British satirical puppet show, 'Spitting Image', which has usually contented itself with lampooning politicians and the Royal Family, finally brought out a 'Jesus'-puppet designed to shock and offend. And the well-known American writer Gore Vidal, in similar vein, published a scurrilous novel about the origins of Christianity, called *Live from Golgotha*, in which, as the editor of *The Times* put it, he came across like a smutty schoolboy shouting rude words across the playground.

It is important to say right from the outset that Christians do not seek a safe haven, protected from this sort of thing. Christianity takes its place in the marketplace of ideas, and is open to public scrutiny and debate. Jesus himself, on the strictly orthodox view, laid himself wide open to misunderstanding, ridicule, abuse and even death. The church has no vested interest in preventing people coming up with new ideas about Jesus. Indeed, I shall myself be arguing later on that, to this extent, the first three authors are right: the real, historical Jesus still has many surprises in store for institutional Christianity.

It is precisely for that reason that I wish to reply to these three books. They address the right issue, namely, who Jesus really was – as opposed to who the church has imagined him to be. But I believe they fail to reach anything like the right answer.

How should one reply? An older generation of controversialists used to quote passage after passage and then rebut them. This is tedious, and I shall not attempt it.

Another method is to write books which clearly demonstrate better ways of looking at the whole area, so that alternative perspectives are simply outflanked. That, I hope, will be part of the effect of my longer, more scholarly works. My book *The Climax of the Covenant* (T. & T. Clark, 1991) sets out a way of reading Paul which, I submit, makes far more sense than Wilson's or Spong's crucial chapters on the apostle. My recent book *The New Testament and the People of God* (SPCK, 1992) sets out a detailed argument about the nature of history, and about first-century Judaism and early Christianity, which cuts the ground from under a good deal of all three books discussed here. In what follows (e.g. the discussions of the gospels, and of the resurrection) I shall often be drawing on this work, which is abbreviated in the Notes as *NTPG*.

My forthcoming book *Jesus and the Victory of God* (SPCK, 1993) will set out a detailed and closely-argued case for a way of understanding Jesus in his historical context. This will constitute, by implication, my full positive reply to the three works here discussed; the final chapter of the present book is a tiny sketch of this longer treatment. But there I shall of course take as my conversation partners, not the recent maverick popularizers, but the serious scholarly writers in the field, particularly Vermes, Meyer, Harvey, Borg, Sanders, Horsley, Crossan and Meier.

The third way of replying to books like those of Thiering, Wilson and Spong is to show quite briefly the context of discussion in which they belong, the broad lines of their arguments, and the main reasons why they are to be discounted. That is the task of the present book. I am grateful to SPCK for taking it on, and to Andrew Goddard and David Mackinder for reading the manuscript at short notice and making several helpful comments. Though brief, I hope this work will show that it is possible to take current questions seriously and still emerge with a way of understanding Jesus that does justice both to history and to mainstream Christian belief. At the same time, I know that my own understanding of Jesus, and hence of Christianity, has been deeply and profoundly affected by my historical study. Whatever else is the case about my beliefs and my scholarship, it is certainly not true that I have 'found' a 'Jesus' who has merely reinforced the belief-system I had before the process began. The closer I get to Jesus within his historical context, the more I find my previous ideas, and indeed my previous self, radically subverted.

Among other beliefs, I hold more firmly than ever to the conviction that serious study of Jesus and the gospels is best done within the context of a worshipping community. I have been privileged, over the last six years, to minister to the Christian community that meets in Worcester College Chapel, Oxford. They have sustained me with their love, their enthusiasm, their criticism, and their prayers. I dedicate this book to them with much gratitude.

Tom Wright

1

The Portraits and the Puzzles

The Great Revolution

Think of a Victorian drawing-room, hung with faded portraits. They stare down at you: respectable, aloof, worthy, a bit faded. The frames are heavy, gilt-edged, cracked here and there.

Now imagine a man, with wild hair and flashing eyes, bursting into the room. He rushes round, tearing the portraits from the walls as though in a frenzy. He smashes the glass in the frames and tramples on the paintings with his dirty boots. Then, when the walls are bare, he takes from inside his coat a single sheet of paper. On it we see, drawn in rough black crayon, a stark outline of a figure, not unlike himself, with a wild, visionary face. It is the sort of figure to which people are either instinctively drawn or from which they instinctively recoil. He slaps it in the middle of the main wall of the room, so that it hangs by the nail where the chief old portrait had been. Then, in a trice, he is gone. His own vision leads him to further tasks, all equally dramatic.

The man is Albert Schweitzer; the drawing-room is the nineteenth-century European religious world; the old portraits are the studies of Jesus that were written, in great quantity, between the late eighteenth and late nineteenth centuries. The new picture is Schweitzer's own substitute: Jesus the apocalyptic visionary, dreaming dreams, seeing visions, daring the impossible, dying in the attempt, and becoming, by sheer force of personality, the greatest and most haunting human being who ever lived.

Schweitzer's own life-story looms over the twentieth century as Jesus' does across the first. He was a brilliant musician and musicologist; a world-class philosopher, historian and theologian; he became a lifelong pioneer medical missionary in what was then still darkest Africa. He wrote his book *The Quest of the Historical Jesus* in 1906, when he was not yet thirty years

old. To a large extent, it set the agenda and the tone for all subsequent writing about Jesus. In particular, it has posed a set of
puzzles that still await a solution.

In this chapter we shall examine this story of portraits and
puzzles. I have written about all this elsewhere;[1] here I shall be
content to summarize large issues and concentrate on pointing
the first-time reader in the right direction.

We need, first, to look at the old portraits, and see why it was
that someone, sooner or later, was bound to rip them off the
walls. Then we shall look at the effect of Schweitzer's action on
subsequent thinking (what does a family *do* when its faded but
cherished past is destroyed before its eyes?). Then, bringing us
up to date, we shall study a little more closely the serious work
that has been going on for the last twenty years or so, and which
sets the context for present and future writing about Jesus. The
family, we shall discover, has started to come to terms with the
great revolution, and has cautiously begun to produce some
more portraits. If, at the end of the day, we conclude that
Schweitzer was wrong, but in precisely the right way, that may be
exactly the sort of homage that he would have desired.

The Old Portraits

Reimarus

First, the old portraits. A little over two hundred years ago, the
German sceptic H. S. Reimarus (1694–1768) declared that if we
were to ask serious historical questions about Jesus, we would
discover that Christianity was based on a mistake. Jesus was not
a 'divine' figure; he was a Jewish revolutionary, who died a failure. His disciples stole his body; then they wrote stories about
him which made him out to be the great redeemer, expected by
the Jews, who would appear on the clouds of heaven and bring
the world to an end. That didn't happen, either; but their early
belief was adapted, not least by Paul, into forms which enabled
it to spread throughout the gullible ancient world. We today,
said Reimarus, can see that the whole thing was a tissue of lies.

Thus began the so-called 'Quest for (or 'of') the historical
Jesus'. Reimarus' theory is actually quite like that of A. N. Wilson in our own day; Wilson's Jesus is not a revolutionary (he is a

bit too bland for that), but in other respects the story looks similar. One of the first things to get straight in the current debate, certainly at the 'popular' level represented by Wilson and others, is that the questions that are being raised are emphatically not new. Despite universal education in the Western world, the news media are still able to maintain that some writer or other has come up with a devastating new discovery or theory which represents a significant challenge to Christianity. Again and again these turn out to be variations on well-worn themes, of which Reimarus' was simply one of the early ones.

D. F. Strauss

The first hundred years or so of the 'quest', covering basically the nineteenth century, consisted largely of attacks on orthodoxy by sceptics, and replies from the orthodox side. The greatest of the nineteenth-century sceptics was David Friedrich Strauss (whose book, interestingly enough, was translated into English by the novelist George Eliot). Strauss (1808–74) amplified Reimarus' scepticism, arguing that most of the stories the gospels told, particularly the 'miracles', were simply untrue. They were 'myths'. By this problematic word Strauss meant (a) that they didn't actually happen and (b) that they were projections, on to the screen of a fictitious 'past', of the beliefs of the early church. Since, for Strauss, the faith that really mattered had nothing much to do with history, he thought that Christianity in some form or other could be rescued from the débâcle brought about by his straightforward denial of the 'miraculous'. None the less, Strauss' work was felt as a threat by many ordinary Christians.

Renan

A very different form of scepticism can be seen in the work of the Frenchman Ernest Renan (1823–92). His romantic portrait of Jesus was typical of many nineteenth-century writings, whose influence lingers on not least through many dreamy but dreary pre-Raphaelite paintings. For Renan, Jesus was the great moral teacher and example, who won the hearts of the masses in the 'Galilean springtime' of the early ministry, only to lose support when his demands became too rigorous. But Jesus' eternal message outlasts his failure, even though the church has muddled it up and turned it into a system and a hierarchy. Despite the fact that nobody today takes Renan seriously as a historian, there are clear echoes of him in some of the recent writings about Jesus.

Holtzmann

Jesus the Teacher of Timeless Ethical Truths was the result of a much more thoroughgoing work by the leading German scholar H. J. Holtzmann (1832–1910). His book focused particular attention on the synoptic gospels (i.e. Matthew, Mark and Luke). He believed that if we could solve the problem of their mutual relationship we could in principle find our way back, as historians, to Jesus. He came up with the solution, now widely accepted, that Mark's gospel was the first of the three to be written. He argued (this, however, is not so widely accepted) that it was therefore the most accurate. The theory of 'Markan priority' thus emerged from the need, among reasonably orthodox Christians, to answer Strauss. Make Mark first, and you will appear to show that the documentation for Jesus' ministry is in fact good; it cannot be dismissed as late fabrication. Holtzmann thus put on to the agenda of Jesus-study the question of the gospels and their nature, and the fact that studying the gospels and studying Jesus are closely interrelated.

Weiss

Another highly significant element was added to the Quest by Johannes Weiss (1863–1914). Faced with an understanding of 'the Kingdom of God' in Jesus' teaching which reduced it to terms of a generalized and liberal ethic (as though Jesus simply went about telling people to be nice to each other), Weiss stubbornly insisted that the phrase 'Kingdom of God' meant something quite different in first-century Judaism. There it referred, he said, not to general religious or ethical ideals, but to the belief that God would shortly step into history and bring the whole world to an end. The question of Jewish 'eschatology' (that is, beliefs about the coming End), and of whether Jesus taught something like it, have continued to dominate subsequent discussions.

Schweitzer

All these writers, and many more for whom there is no space here, were brilliantly described by Albert Schweitzer in the book already referred to, *The Quest of the Historical Jesus*. Schweitzer had little difficulty in showing that a great deal of writing about Jesus was simply imaginative fantasy. 'The Jesus of Nazareth who . . . preached the ethic of the Kingdom of God, who founded the Kingdom of Heaven upon earth, never had any existence.'[2] The old portraits had had their day. Instead, Schweitzer took his cue from Weiss, and built up his own quite startling sketch of Jesus as an apocalyptic prophet.

Jesus, he said, expected the coming of the 'Kingdom of God' – that is, the end of the world – within a very short time. He believed that he was the Messiah (not, it should be noted, that he was 'divine'), but told his disciples to keep this a secret. Judas, however, betrayed the secret to the chief priests, who had Jesus arrested and crucified. Jesus understood his forthcoming death in terms of the old Jewish belief that Israel would pass through a period of great suffering before the Kingdom would come. He believed, according to Schweitzer, that he would have to pass this way himself, alone.

As in some of the portraits, Schweitzer's Jesus died a failure. The world did not end. The Kingdom did not come. Yet the death of those timebound hopes meant the liberation of the real message of Jesus, whose towering 'personality' now looms over all times and places, a strange, unknown, brooding presence, summoning people everywhere to fresh tasks.

Schweitzer thus drew together many of the strands of what is now known as the 'Old Quest'. Like Reimarus, he believed that Jesus was to be understood within his Jewish context, and that within that context he seems to have been a failure. Like Strauss, he believed that he could rescue from the ruins a timeless message which the accidents of history could not damage. Like Weiss, he saw that the Jewish context into which Jesus was to be

fitted was that of 'apocalyptic' expectation, by which he meant
the (supposedly) Jewish belief that the world was very shortly
going to come to an end. Like a great many writers before and
since, Schweitzer believed that the real, 'historical' Jesus should
be allowed to challenge the 'Jesus' of the churches, who had
often been a tamed and domesticated version of the real thing.
Although Schweitzer is commonly reckoned to have brought the
'Old Quest' to an end, these central elements survived through
his own work, and all remain of vital importance in the contemporary 'Quest'.

**Recovering from the Shock:
Schweitzer to Bultmann and Beyond**

History and Faith

Schweitzer's sketch of Jesus was so unpalatable that a great
many people refused to accept it. Since, however, it was
apparently based on thorough historical scholarship, the only
way that serious people could get round it was by denying that
the question of 'who Jesus really was' could have any great significance. The scholars (it was felt) had produced a maze of different 'Jesus' figures, none of whom corresponded to the Christ
worshipped in the church; therefore, so much the worse for the
scholars. Schweitzer's protest against the 'official' Jesus in the
name of the 'historical' one rebounded against him.

The sixty years after Schweitzer saw this split widen into a
deep gulf, with history on one side and faith on the other. It is
ironic, when this same split is heralded on the cover of A. N.
Wilson's new book as though it were a sudden radical discovery,
to find that it wasn't a new idea even at the turn of the century.
The idea goes back at least as far as the eighteenth-century
German philosopher Lessing, who, significantly enough, was the
man who saw to it that Reimarus' work on Jesus got published.

Archbishop William Temple, as a young man, once asked his
father why the philosophers did not apparently rule the world.
The answer ('Of course they do, silly – two hundred years after
they die') has come emphatically true in the case of Lessing.
Today, millions of people who have never heard his name

believe implicitly that between history and faith there is, in Lessing's own phrase, 'a nasty big ditch'.[3]

Barth and Bultmann

This 'ditch' is sometimes regarded as a threat to Christian theology, but it was the theologians who appealed to it in the wake of Schweitzer's work. It appeared in a mild form in the writings of Martin Kähler in 1892, and was then taken up by the great scholars Karl Barth (1886–1968) and Rudolf Bultmann (1884–1976). They argued that a 'life of Jesus', such as the nineteenth century had envisaged, simply could not be written; that the 'personality' of Jesus, on which Schweitzer had laid so much stress, could not be discovered from the sources; and that, in any case, what one might or might not discover about Jesus' historical situation was of no interest whatever for theology. Insofar as we could know anything about Jesus (Bultmann did write a short book about him), he turns out to have been simply a preacher of the timeless call for decision.

Barth and Bultmann together were largely responsible for the fact that in the first half of the twentieth century serious work on the 'quest' hardly existed. (If we cannot have our nice old portraits, we will studiously ignore the crude sketch that has replaced them.) Instead, a good deal of attention was focused on the gospels, and on the traditions of Jesus-stories which had circulated orally prior to being written down.

Study of the Gospels

This period (roughly 1910–60) saw the rise of 'form criticism', the study of the forms of individual paragraphs in the gospels (parables, miracle-stories, and so forth) with a view to establishing their use in different early Christian settings. This method has often been referred to as part of the 'quest for Jesus' itself. Properly, however, it belongs to a period in which people were not so much trying to find out about Jesus himself as trying to understand the faith of the earliest church, as *expressed in* its telling of Jesus-stories. It was simply assumed that we could know little about the 'real' Jesus that would be of value to faith.

This focus of study on the gospels drew out, then, one element of the older 'quest' to which Schweitzer had given less attention, namely, the nature of the gospels. Are they history, myth, or what? What is their relationship to each other, and what does that tell us about their reliability? These questions have not gone away. Recent study has confirmed their central importance. Schweitzer had assumed that the gospels gave us, more or less, information about Jesus, even if we had to do some sorting of wheat from chaff and some rearranging of episodes into their proper chronological order. As he himself knew, there was an alternative way of reading them, which in his day had just been pioneered by the Dutchman William Wrede: Mark, used as a main source by the other gospels, is a theological fiction, which cannot be trusted to give us information about Jesus, but only about Mark's own theology.[4] The question at issue between Schweitzer and Wrede remains on the table to this day. Is Jesus a first-century Jewish prophet, or are the gospels simply fiction?

The So-Called 'New Quest'

Käsemann's Initiative

On 20 October 1953, Professor Ernst Käsemann, an erstwhile pupil of Bultmann, delivered a lecture in which he effectively got the 'quest' going again. He was careful to agree with the Barth/Bultmann line: a 'life of Jesus' could not be written. But he argued strongly that the 'Christ' who is worshipped by the church must be firmly attached to the real Jesus who lived in Palestine in the first century, and who died on a cross. Without that attachment, the word 'Jesus' becomes a mere cipher. We can pull and push it this way or that without any control. 'Jesus' can be invoked to support all kinds of programmes. To prevent this, we need serious Jesus-research.

Criteria for Jesus-Research?

But how is Jesus-research to be done? In the 1950s and 1960s there was much debate about the different 'criteria' which were available for assessing whether this or that saying of Jesus was 'authentic' or not. This became one of the keynotes of the 'new quest': (a) a concentration on *sayings* rather than *deeds* of Jesus, and (b) the proliferation of debate about criteria for authenticity. Among the suggestions have been the following.

(a) A saying of Jesus is considered likely to be original if it is 'dissimilar', that is, unlike anything found in contemporary Judaism or in the early church. An example might be Jesus' command to 'leave the dead to bury their dead' (Matthew 8.22). Such sayings are unlikely to have been well-known Jewish sayings, or to reflect suspiciously some interest of primitive Christianity. This 'criterion of dissimilarity' has been attacked on the rather obvious grounds that sayings discovered by such means are unlikely to have been central to Jesus' purpose. He was, after all, working in a Jewish setting, and the church did claim to be following his teaching, not inventing something new.

(b) 'Multiple attestation' occurs if a saying is found in more than one strand of tradition (one gospel, or one source). This sounds fine until it is actually applied; for in any given case, if a saying is found in two different places, some critic somewhere will claim that one of the passages depends on the other.

(c) 'Consistency' occurs if a saying seems to fit well in tone and theology with one that has already been established as probably authentic. This again makes good sense, but obviously leads one into a circle. Where should we break in, and why?

(d) Linguistic and cultural tests are sometimes advanced to show that a saying fits; or does not fit, into the Aramaic-speaking world of Jesus and into the complex Jewish culture of his time. An example might be Jesus' famous use of 'Abba' (Father) in prayer. The trouble with this is that proving a negative (i.e. showing that something doesn't fit) is always difficult in ancient history. We simply don't have enough information. Proving a positive verdict is sometimes equally difficult. In particular, this criterion flies in the face of the first one (dissimilarity), which starts by looking for the sayings which do *not* fit into the cultural milieu of the time.

Bornkamm, Schillebeeckx and Jeremias

Works about Jesus written on this basis have, perhaps not surprisingly, proved themselves of little worth, not being taken up much in subsequent discussion. The best-known books in this category are those of G. Bornkamm (*Jesus of Nazareth*[5]) and E. Schillebeeckx (*Jesus: An Experiment in Christology*[6]). Of perhaps more lasting value, though also largely ignored in a good deal of contemporary work, is the first volume of Joachim Jeremias' uncompleted *New Testament Theology*, entitled *The Proclamation of Jesus*.[7] Jeremias' knowledge of Aramaic enabled him to locate several sayings within a plausible first-century milieu. His interpretation of Jesus' Kingdom-teaching attempted to hold together the belief that the Kingdom was purely future (as Schweitzer had thought) and the belief that it was in some sense already present (as had been argued strongly by the English writer C. H. Dodd in a number of works[8]).

The 'Jesus Seminar'

A few years ago, it looked as if this 'New Quest' was running into a dead end. As we shall see, several scholars had begun to ask questions about Jesus in a quite different way. But recently it has had a new lease of life, in the American 'Jesus Seminar', organized by Professor Robert Funk. This group consists of scholars from across North America, who come together to discuss the sayings of Jesus one by one, and then to vote on their authenticity. They are given four options: certainly inauthentic, probably inauthentic, probably authentic, certainly authentic. This method has been much mocked, but at least it concentrates the mind. Whether the results that will eventually emerge will be worth any more than anyone else's, or whether they will be seen simply as another projection of various ideologies, remains to be seen.

Mack and Crossan

Within the 'Jesus Seminar', and notably in the publications of two of its members (Burton Mack and Dominic Crossan), one strand of opinion has argued quite strongly that the best model for the real historical Jesus is that of the wandering Cynic preacher. (The 'Cynics' were self-appointed rugged individuals who wandered the Roman empire preaching a severe version of the popular Stoic philosophy, and gathering disciples with similar intent.) In Mack's treatment,[9] this has the following effect. The oldest parts of the gospel tradition turn out to be the apparently non-Jewish ones, while Jewish ideas are regarded as later intrusions into the tradition. The process culminates in Mark's gospel, which, according to Mack, created a 'myth' of Jesus' heroic life. This corresponded to nothing in actual history. Nevertheless, it launched the church into a new and (for Mack) disastrous direction. It had started, according to Mack, as a fairly disorganized movement of social protest. Mark turned it into a socially conformist Jewish, and anti-world, organization.

Dominic Crossan's reconstruction is one of the most brilliant works to emerge from recent study of Jesus.[10] Like some other brilliant works, however, it arguably overreaches itself. Certainly the publisher's bold claim on the jacket of the book ('The first comprehensive determination of who Jesus was, what he did, what he said') seems to be asking for trouble. Crossan, in fact, knows perfectly well that all history is *interpreted* history: he does not, in the book itself, claim more for his theory than that it is just that, one possible theory.

Crossan spends a good deal of time arguing for a particular understanding of the world in which Jesus lived. He draws on some sociological studies to present a hypothetical picture of peasant society in the Mediterranean world, and then of the specifically Jewish form of that kind of culture. Into this he places Jesus, as a shrewd peasant teacher who challenged all the existing forms and patterns of social order. Jesus kept on the move, refusing to make himself the centre of his own message. He simply encouraged people to enter what Crossan calls a 'brokerless kingdom of God', that is, a state of being in which each individual enjoys unmediated access to God. Jesus is thus a Jewish 'Cynic' in the sense outlined above.

In order to reach this conclusion, Crossan makes a basic move which, in terms of the history of the subject, is quite breathtaking. To understand this, we need to backtrack a little.

Almost all other researchers have assumed that our basic information about Jesus comes from Matthew, Mark and Luke, with a bit here and there from John. The material about Jesus which appears among the gnostic collections discovered at Nag Hammadi in Egypt in 1945 is normally regarded as a much later product, and hence strictly secondary.

Crossan reverses all this. For him, the 'Gospel of Thomas' – a collection of 'sayings of Jesus', some of which are quite obviously 'gnostic' – is one of our earliest sources.[11] Another is a version of 'Q', a hypothetical document supposed to lie behind Matthew and Luke. Some scholars have spent ages trying to reconstruct 'Q'; others don't believe it ever existed. Crossan assumes it did. He thinks he can detect which bits of it were the earliest. And (perhaps unsurprisingly) they just happen to look rather like some bits of the 'Gospel of Thomas'.

Crossan's Jesus is thus very different from Matthew's, Mark's or Luke's. Like Wrede at the beginning of the century, Crossan thinks that Mark and the others completely falsified Jesus. Like Burton Mack, he thinks the true portrait was covered up by a Jewish re-reading of the Jesus-story, a story which hadn't originally been so very Jewish, but was more in line with movements in the pagan world of the time. Jesus thus turns out to be a cross between a 'Gnostic' and a 'Cynic'.

It remains to be seen whether this portrait of 'Jesus' will commend itself to those outside the charmed circle of the 'Jesus Seminar' and others within what remains of the 'New Quest'. It is a brilliant piece of work, but remains highly speculative and contentious.

It is my judgment that this 'New Quest' has in fact produced little of lasting value. It got European scholarship going again on the trail of Jesus. However, it remained stuck in post-Bultmannian anguish about whether we could really find out anything about Jesus, and even about whether we ought to try. For myself, I think the future lies elsewhere, in what I have called the 'Third Quest'. To this we now turn.

The 'Third Quest': Vermes to Sanders and Beyond

Schweitzer brought down the curtain on the 'Old Quest'. The 'New Quest' has rumbled on for nearly thirty years without producing much in the way of solid results. Now, in the last twenty years or so, we have had a quite different movement, which has emerged without anyone co-ordinating it and without any particular theological agenda, but with a definite shape none the less. I have called this the 'Third Quest'.

One of the most obvious features of this 'Third Quest' has been the bold attempt to set Jesus firmly into his Jewish context. Another feature has been that, unlike the 'New Quest', the writers I shall mention have largely ignored the artificial pseudo-historical 'criteria' for different sayings in the gospels. Instead, they have offered complete hypotheses about Jesus' whole life and work, including not only sayings but also deeds. This has made for a more complete, and less artificial, historical flavour to the whole enterprise.

Brandon and Vermes

Two early writers in this vein were S. G. F. Brandon and G. Vermes.[12] Brandon revived the thesis of Reimarus, according to which Jesus was really a Jewish revolutionary. Vermes suggested that he was simply a Galilean *hasid*, a holy man. Both did much to jolt Jesus-studies out of their preoccupation with potential theological significance and into the real world of first-century Palestine.

Unfortunately for Brandon's argument, it has proved impossible to sustain the idea of 'Jesus the revolutionary'. The evidence is massively against it.[13] Unfortunately for Vermes, the shock value of his title (*Jesus the Jew*) has faded, as many others have also written about Jesus the Jew without coming to anything like the same conclusions as he did. (A. N. Wilson, who follows Vermes closely, is an exception.) Vermes' theory about Jesus' use of the phrase 'Son of Man', though, has had a long run for its money: he argued that the phrase simply meant 'I' or 'me', and that sentences which couldn't be reduced to this weren't said by Jesus. Neither Brandon's work nor Vermes', seen from twenty years on, has proved to be more than one milestone in the ongoing debate.

The milestone, however, has been significant in itself. Brandon and Vermes forced scholarship to look back to what Schweitzer was trying to say in his own way: if we are to understand Jesus, it must be within, not simply over against, first-century Judaism. Schweitzer saw this in terms of apocalyptic; Brandon, in terms of revolution; Vermes, in terms of Jewish piety. There is a sense in which all were right, though all need supplementing, not just by each other, but by yet more factors within the complex Jewish world of the first century.

Meyer

The writers I regard as most significant within the 'Third Quest' are Ben F. Meyer, Anthony E. Harvey, Marcus J. Borg, and, perhaps particularly, Ed P. Sanders.[14] Each in his own way manages to set Jesus quite credibly within his first-century Jewish context. Each advances a more or less complete hypothesis, rather than attempting to pick at individual sayings or incidents.

There is in this movement an increasing sophistication in the use of literary and historical methods. This can be seen particularly in Ben Meyer's book *The Aims of Jesus*. In a long introduction, he not only sheds new light on the philosophical and theological roots of the 'Quests', old and new, but also suggests a fresh approach to our knowledge of Jesus, based on the distinction between the 'outside' and the 'inside' of historical events. The 'outside' is 'what happened', while the 'inside' has to do with the all-important motivation of the characters. It makes sense to ask, in relation to any historical event, *why* the characters did what they did.

On this basis, Meyer offers a painstaking reconstruction of Jesus' aims. In public, he announced the Kingdom of God, for which Israel had been longing. In private, with the disciples, the question of Jesus' own messianic identity could emerge. Jesus envisaged himself as the founder of a new, messianic community, a reborn Israel. The church which emerged from Jesus' work does not represent a significant shift away from his real intention, but rather a completion, a carrying on in a new situation, of what he had begun. It is a pity that Meyer's work, at once both brilliant and cautious, a model of wise and patient scholarship, has not had more impact on the recent spate of popular writing about Jesus.

Harvey

Anthony Harvey's Bampton Lectures, given in Oxford in 1980, are just as fresh and creative in terms of method. Harvey argues that we can deduce certain things about Jesus in terms of 'historical constraint'. In any given historical situation there are certain things which will make sense, and certain others which will not. If, then, we start with a clear understanding of the historical setting of Jesus' ministry, we will be able to deduce that Jesus 'must' have acted in certain ways. Perhaps the most impressive application of this argument is in terms of the crucifixion. Harvey argues that, in the light of our knowledge of Jewish and Roman law, the bare fact that Jesus was crucified should lead us to the conclusion that the events which led up to that moment must have been substantially as the four canonical gospels record them. This, too, is an argument that has not been taken with sufficient seriousness in some recent writing.

Borg

The great achievement of Marcus Borg, in my judgment, is to have demonstrated that the severe warnings which the gospels attribute to Jesus have little or nothing to do with either hell-fire after death or with the end of the world, in the sense of the end of the space-time universe. Instead, the warnings are to be read as typical pieces of Jewish 'apocalyptic' language, as prophecies about a *this-worldly* judgment which is to be *interpreted as* the judgment of Israel's God.

This means that Jesus, for Borg, was emphatically 'political'. Not in the sense that he wanted to lead a military revolt. To the contrary: Jesus opposed the nationalistic militarism which was sweeping Israel at the time. As a result, he also opposed those religious systems which focused on an exclusive holiness, setting Israel up against her pagan neighbours, and exalting the outwardly righteous within Israel over against the poor and the outcasts. Instead, Jesus advocated the practice of *mercy* as the true form of imitating God, and hence of holiness. This was 'political' in that Jesus was opposing both the powerful vested interests in Jewish society and also the movements for revolt.

Borg is thus able to take the evidence upon which Schweitzer based his arguments, and turn it in a very different direction. The great imminent event was not the end of the world as such, but a coming national disaster. Jerusalem, and the Temple, would fall before enemy attack. This re-reading of 'apocalyptic' language is yet another element which has yet to make its impact in popular-level writing about Jesus: certainly Thiering, Wilson and Spong do not seem to have taken any notice of it.

Sanders

Ed Sanders begins his treatment of Jesus, unusually but very effectively, by discussing Jesus' action in the Temple. Jesus' motivation, he argues, was not to 'cleanse' the Temple of corrupt practices, but to announce its imminent judgment. (At this point Sanders is close to Borg.) Like some other Jewish groups, including the authors of the Scrolls, Jesus regarded the present Temple system as hopelessly corrupt, and believed that the only solution was for it to be destroyed, and a new one put up in its place. It was this opposition to the Temple, Sanders believes, which set in motion the events that led to Jesus' death.

Unlike Borg, Sanders does not believe that Jesus had any real controversy with the Pharisees, as the gospels suggest. There are isolated sayings, he allows, which would have sounded odd, even shocking, in Jewish ears (e.g. 'Leave the dead to bury their dead'); but most of the sharp discussions, for instance about the food laws or the sabbath, come from a later period, after the church and synagogue had split from one another. Jesus himself would not have spoken against the Jewish Torah in that way, and, even if he had, debates on such issues would not have led to violence, merely to more debate.

Sanders is in some ways the clearest of the recent writers on Jesus. His work has been used in some of the recent popular writing, not least by Wilson; but the full impact that its thorough scholarship deserves is yet to be felt at pew-level, let alone at street-level. Sanders is candid about the issues he leaves unresolved, or even undiscussed. Thus, for instance, he offers no solution to the vexed problem of whether Jesus spoke of the 'Son of Man', and if so what he might have meant by it. Again, he speaks of the disciples following through Jesus' agenda 'in a changed situation'. But he does not venture a hypothesis about what precisely 'changed' the situation, between (that is) Jesus' death and the rise of the early church. At these and other points we may well feel that we want both to go beyond him and to challenge some of his conclusions. But his book on Jesus remains a major contribution to the Quest.

Issues from the Third Quest

There are many other writers whose work has to be taken seriously in any attempt to get to grips with what is really happening in modern Jesus-studies. I have discussed those that seem to me to be the most significant, whose work has yet to have its full impact across the gamut of scholarship.[15] Taken together, their work propels us forward to ask certain key questions, which in my opinion are legitimate and serious from anyone's point of view. They are as follows:

First, what was Jesus' relationship with the Judaism of his day? At what points did he share the aspirations of his contemporaries; at what point did he challenge them? In particular, what did he say and do that related to Jewish hopes for the immediate future?

Second, what were Jesus' actual aims? Christianity has often spoken of Jesus as though he simply had the lofty aim of saving the world by dying for it; but, whether or not that is plausible (we must return to this later), what were the aims and motivations that led him on in his day-to-day ministry? What (to turn the question the other way round) was he wanting people to *do* if they were to respond to him appropriately?

Third, why did Jesus die? A spectrum of opinion becomes visible at this point. At one end there is Jesus-the-revolutionary; of course the Romans killed him, as they would any other revolutionary leader. The problem is that none of our sources makes Jesus look remotely like a revolutionary leader. At the other end of the spectrum is the bland Jesus, the mild Jesus, the Jesus who was so thoroughly like any other ordinary Jewish holy man that it is hard to see why anyone would have wanted to oppose him, let alone crucify him. Somewhere in between these two extremes the truth must lie; but where? And, in particular: did Jesus believe himself called to meet a violent death as part of his vocation? (Other Jews, we should note, had thought of themselves in this way before.)

Fourth, why did the early church begin? This is, of course, another way of asking the question: what really happened at

Easter? Here the 'Third Quest' has had, so far, little to say; but
serious historical research cannot remain silent here of all
places. The theories offered at this point in recent popular writing such as that of Thiering and Wilson are, frankly, laughable.
What are the serious alternatives?

Fifth, why are the gospels what they are? We may grant, of
course, that they are written by Christians and (largely though
not, perhaps, exclusively) for Christians. So what? Are they, like
the better newspapers, substantially true but slanted? Or are
they, like the worse newspapers, substantially slanted and largely
untrue? Or what? What genre are they? What does that tell us,
not only about their authors, but about Jesus?

These, I suggest, are the questions that ought now to be
addressed in serious historical study of Jesus. They are also the
starting-point for serious *theological* study of Jesus. It will not do,
as we have seen many writers try to do, to separate the historical
from the theological. 'Jesus' is either the flesh-and-blood individual who walked and talked, and lived and died, in first-
century Palestine, or he is merely a creature of our own imagination, able to be manipulated this way and that.

To this extent, I totally agree with the proposals of the sceptical 'questers', from Reimarus right down to A. N. Wilson. It is
not only possible, but actually highly likely, that the church has
distorted the real Jesus, and needs to repent of this and rediscover who its Lord actually is. But this does not mean that the
church has been wrong in everything it has said about Jesus.
Only real no-holds-barred history can tell us whether that is so.
My argument from this point onwards will *not* be that Thiering,
Wilson and Spong have offered a historical Jesus which the
church must resist in the name of its cherished traditional faith.
It *will* be that they have offered us a Jesus of their own imagination, which the church, and anyone else who may be interested,
ought to resist in the name of serious history.

This serious history will, of course, challenge some forms of
Christian faith. Christians are not particularly free from muddles
and misconceptions, any more than anyone else is. But, when all
is said and done, Christianity ought to emerge from historical
enquiry more solid and robust, not watered down or thinned out.
Instead of bad portraits, we need good ones.

2

Barbara Thiering: Jesus in Code

A Strange New Theory

Of all the books I have ever read about Jesus, Barbara Thiering's is one of the strangest. Entitled *Jesus the Man: A New Interpretation from the Dead Sea Scrolls*, it has been marketed vigorously in its native Australia and on both sides of the Atlantic. The most distinctive thing about the book, which has guaranteed it headlines all round the globe, is the suggestion that Jesus was married (to Mary Magdalene – might one have guessed?); that he had three children, a daughter and two sons, by her; that they then divorced, and that Jesus married again.

In this book, as in all her writings, Thiering makes extensive use of the Dead Sea Scrolls. In recent years there has been a great deal of media attention to these priceless documents, which were discovered in 1947 in caves near the shore of the Dead Sea, about fifteen miles from Jerusalem. Journalists in search of a sensational story have again and again tried to make out that the Scrolls have pulled the rug out from under traditional Christianity. It is sometimes even alleged that much of the contents of the Scrolls was kept secret by the Christian scholars who had taken charge of them, for fear lest word would leak out that the foundations of the church were being undermined.[1]

Yet it has been made clear, time and again, by serious scholars from all backgrounds – Jewish, Christian, and those of other religions or none – that this is not the case. The Scrolls remain one of the most fascinating and valuable sets of documents, providing us with a huge amount of information about a breakaway Jewish sect that was in existence between roughly 150 BC and AD 70. But nobody at the serious scholarly level has imagined that they actually mention Christianity itself.

Nobody, that is, except Barbara Thiering. She thinks that the Scrolls provide a good deal of evidence about Christianity, and

conversely that the gospels provide a good deal of evidence
about the community that wrote the Scrolls. How this comes
about we will explore in a minute.

Thiering herself is anxious about the over-emphasis that the
media have placed on the inevitably sensational ideas about
Jesus' marital and family life. When I met her for a live discussion on the ITN lunchtime news programme (Monday, 14 September 1992), she was irritated that the interviewer highlighted
precisely these features of her book. They were not, she claimed,
the central points. Yet it is undeniable that they are the feature
which has guaranteed the book such extraordinary publicity.

Previous Works

The 'Teacher of Righteousness'

In addition, it is also clear that these ideas about Jesus' family
life are the only really 'new' thing about her new book. Thiering
had previously published her main argument in three more
apparently scholarly works.[2] The first was *Redating the Teacher
of Righteousness*, published in 1979. The 'Teacher of Righteousness' is a shadowy figure who is mentioned several times in the
Dead Sea Scrolls, and is pretty clearly one of the founders, or at
any rate one of the great early leaders, of the sect who produced
the Scrolls. Almost all scholars have placed this 'teacher' in the
second century BC.[3] Thiering puts him in the first century AD –
and identifies him with John the Baptist, whom of course we
know from the gospels. Despite a great deal of scholarly work on
the Scrolls since this book was published, not one single recognized authority has found this argument convincing. This can't
be put down to Christian prejudice: most of the authorities in
question are either Jewish or agnostic.

The Gospels in Code?

Thiering's second book was entitled *The Gospels and Qumran: A
New Hypothesis*. In this work, published in 1981, she argued that
the gospels were written in a code which we could now crack

with the aid of the Scrolls. This is one of the crucial points in her theory, and needs explaining a little further.

The people who wrote the Scrolls believed that all the prophecies of the Hebrew Bible (our Old Testament) had started to come true at last. The fact that their communal life didn't look exactly like what the prophets had said was a minor problem, and they solved it as follows. The prophets, they said, were giving secret divine revelation, to which they, the community, now had the key. They could therefore read a book of prophecy and *interpret* it, line by line, to refer to themselves.

The way this works is as follows. The Hebrew for 'interpretation' is the word *pesher*. Suppose we take the book of Habakkuk. In chapter 2 verse 8 we find the words: 'because of the blood of men and the violence done to the land, to the city, and to all its inhabitants'. The Scroll which comments on Habakkuk quotes this passage, and then says: 'Interpreted [i.e. *pesher*], this concerns the Wicked Priest whom God delivered into the hands of his enemies because of the iniquity committed against the Teacher of Righteousness.'[4] This sets the pattern: first a quote from Scripture, then an 'interpretation' (*'pesher'*), applying what was said long ago to the present context and community.

So far, so good. All scholars agree that this is indeed how several of the Scrolls 'work'. But at this point Thiering introduces a totally new idea. The same community, she suggests, also wrote its own present story in code, intending a similar method of 'pesher' to be used in reading the actual historical reality out of a coded text.

Where is this coded history of the community to be found? In the gospels. The clue, says Thiering, is that the gospels contain plenty of reference to 'supernatural' happenings – miracles, angelic visits, and so forth. These, she says, are the vital places where bits and pieces of the community's history lie buried. Once we learn the 'pesher' technique, we can read these stories as what they really are: coded community history.

Once again, it is fair to say that this theory, which was put before the scholarly world over a decade ago, has convinced no one, whether Jewish, Christian or agnostic, with any pretensions to Scrolls scholarship. Nevertheless, it is the vital basis for the entire enterprise of the new book *Jesus the Man*.

The Scrolls and the Church

Thiering's third book built on the first two. It branched out to
expound her full position – all, that is, except for the bits about
Mary Magdalene, Jesus' three children, and the divorce. In *The
Qumran Origins of the Christian Church*, published in 1983, she
used the identification of John the Baptist with the Teacher of
Righteousness, and the 'pesher' method of reading the gospels,
to sketch a totally new picture of Jesus and early Christianity.

Jesus was, it seems, the 'Wicked Priest' who opposed John the
Baptist (the 'Teacher of Righteousness') and founded his own
branch of the Essene sect (the 'Essenes', it is widely agreed,
were the group who wrote the Scrolls). Stories about 'healings',
and especially about Jesus raising people from the dead, are
code for his promoting people within the community. The
gospels turn out to provide the history of a community that is
strictly organized according to monastic disciplines, with complex initiation ceremonies, precise hours of prayer, exact hierar-
chies, elaborate rituals, and all the trappings of a highly
developed and tight-knit organization. There are even 'Popes'
and 'Cardinals'. (Has Thiering never heard of anachronisms?)
Within this movement, Thiering argues, there were all sorts of
internal political wranglings, which emerge – as always, heavily
coded – in the gospels.

In the middle of it all, Jesus was crucified – not in Jerusalem
itself, but at Qumran, where the community kept its base. He
didn't die on the cross, but was drugged. He was then put in a
cave, along with the two others who were crucified with him.
These two, it appears, are not nameless 'thieves', as in the
gospels. They are Judas Iscariot, whom of course we know from
the gospels, and Simon Magus, who turns up in Acts. They had
had their legs broken, but they didn't die either. Simon Magus,
who had some medical knowledge, was able to administer to
Jesus an antidote to the poison he had taken on the cross. The
antidote, conveniently, consisted of the aloes (spices) which the
women had placed in the tomb. Jesus thus re-emerged, having
apparently 'died' and been raised.

Jesus then, it seems, accompanied his followers, including
Peter and Paul, on various trips round the Mediterranean, so
that when (for instance) Peter received his 'vision' in Acts 10 we
are to understand that Jesus himself was on the roof of the

house and gave Peter a sign of what he should do next. Jesus himself then died some time in the 60s AD.

Once again, it is safe to say that no serious scholar has given this elaborate and fantastic theory any credence whatsoever. It is nearly ten years since it was published; the scholarly world has been able to have a good look at it; and the results are totally negative. The only scholar who takes Thiering's theory with any seriousness is Thiering herself. (Even this I began to doubt at various points in her earlier books, before I began on the new one. There were several passages where I couldn't help wondering whether the whole thing might be an elaborate hoax. When I met Thiering herself, however, it seemed that she really did believe it all.)

Jesus the Publicity Stunt

The main points in the new book *Jesus the Man*, then, were all published some time ago, and the reaction from worldwide scholarship has been entirely negative. The only two things which are substantially new are (a) the additional theory that this Jesus was married to Mary Magdalene, had three children, then divorced her and married again; and (b) a large array of lists, charts, diagrams and annotations which together give the book an appearance of scholarship.

Thiering's ideas about Jesus' family life were first broached in an Australian television programme on Palm Sunday 1990. The broadcast generated a storm of protest, in which, as so often, the real issues got submerged under a quite different discussion, of whether it is right to allow people to raise such questions about Jesus. (Once the discussion shifts on to that plane, the whole thing simply degenerates into a shouting match between angry conservatives and angry radicals, which does nobody any good.) The event quickly attracted the attention of eager publishers, who evidently persuaded Thiering to revise her earlier books and present them, including the new suggestions about Jesus' marriage and so on, in a manner more accessible to the ordinary non-scholarly reader.

Thus we find, at several points, that the new book repeats large chunks of the earlier ones, almost word for word. This time, though, it is all broken up into tiny chapters of three or

four pages, and paragraphs of two or three sentences. This
makes the first half of the book extremely easy to read; the second half, with all the diagrams and charts, is not really designed
to be read at all, but only to be referred to.

Thiering claims that her work 'opens up a whole new
understanding of historical Christianity'. If her theory were correct, this would certainly be true. It seems doubtful, though,
whether anyone would ever take Christianity seriously again.
She seems, though, to want to take it seriously. She insists that
what she is doing is taking the non-human 'divine figure' of
Jesus, such as many Christians have imagined him to be, and
bringing him down to earth, making him after all a real human
being. This task, as almost everyone engaged in the scholarly
quest for Jesus would agree, is vital, exciting, attractive and
necessary; but it would be a grave mistake for anyone reading
Thiering's book to think that it can only be done in this particular way. There are, in fact, several key areas in which her entire
theory is open to severe criticism; so much so, in fact, that at
point after point it can be blown down like a rickety house of
cards.

Points in Favour?

What, if anything, can be said for Thiering's whole scheme?
First, it is right and proper, as I have insisted throughout, to look
for the real human Jesus as he actually was within his historical
context. One answer that has been made to Thiering and others
is that we can never know very much about Jesus, and that
there's no real need to try; but this suggestion, even though
made recently in the columns of *The Times* by Clifford Longley,
its senior Religious Affairs correspondent, is a counsel of
despair.[5] I totally agree with Thiering that we must use all our
historical skill to discover who Jesus really was.

Second, I totally agree that the Dead Sea Scrolls provide vital
and important evidence for the Quest. Whatever they say must
be taken seriously. It is part of the Christian historical task, as
well as the secular or Jewish historical task, to be open to all the
evidence, wherever it comes from. Christians have no need to
hide from history.

Third, it is true, as Thiering emphasizes, that first-century Jews (not only the Essenes, the authors of the Scrolls) were expecting Israel's God to act dramatically within history, and bring about the launch of a worldwide kingdom in which the Gentiles would come to acknowledge the rule of Israel's God. This is often ignored, not least by those who have followed Weiss and Schweitzer in thinking that first-century Jews were expecting the 'end of the world'. In fact, I don't think Thiering herself has taken this Jewish expectation seriously enough.

Fourth, I fully agree with Thiering when she argues that Jesus was offering his Jewish contemporaries a new way of working out what it meant to be the loyal people of God – a way, specifically, that avoided the violence which was so endemic in their society. This seems to me exactly right. But, as we have seen, it is certainly not a new insight.

Fifth, I entirely agree that the church has often muddled up the message of Jesus, and that we need to return to him, not least to find ways of being Christian which highlight his care for the weak and powerless, the sinners and the marginalized. The gospel of Jesus must not be used, as it has often been used, as a weapon of oppression. But to think that Thiering's is the only way of redressing this balance is totally absurd.

There are, then, certain points at which I thoroughly approve of Thiering's aims and intentions. She is right to say that the church has often ignored the real humanity of Jesus and the essential first-century Jewish context within which, and only within which, he and his message can be truly understood. But from here on our paths diverge.

Cracks in the Theory

Scrolls, Essenes and History

One of the most obvious cracks in the structure of Thiering's hypothesis comes fairly near the foundation. The Scrolls, upon which she bases so much, simply weren't written when she says they were. I have scanned the periodical literature and the major recent books on the Scrolls, and at no point do I find scholars dating these documents as late as the first century AD. It is of course possible that the whole world of Scrolls scholarship is wrong, and that Thiering is right. Such things have happened before. But I see no reason, from the arguments she produces, to change the normal view, which is that the events concerning the 'Teacher of Righteousness', the 'Wicked Priest', and so forth, took place some time in the second century BC – i.e. about two hundred years earlier than Thiering makes out.

This of itself would be enough, in fact, to bring the whole structure toppling down. But, since, like all historical arguments, this one has an element of circularity, it is worthwhile to proceed. One of the best arguments that Thiering could possibly produce for her revolutionary late dating would be if, in fact, the rest of the theory made so much sense, and fitted so many things together, that we were compelled to admit that it looked as though, after all, we would have to revise the normal view. This is the argument that Thiering suggests, using the analogy of a jigsaw puzzle: 'The "proof" is in the final success of the method. A clear and integrated picture emerges, leaving no doubt that the whole process was intended' (p. 335). We shall return to this argument at the end of the chapter, and see where it has got us.

'Pesher' and Code

It is, of course, easy to get a historical jigsaw to 'fit' or 'work' if one bit of evidence can 'mean' something else. I suggest that Thiering's use of what she calls 'pesher' functions exactly like this. It is a slippery method which enables her to slide evidence to and fro at will.

To begin with, the 'pesher' method never was, in the Scrolls, a way of writing the history of the community. It was, as we saw, a way of reading ancient prophecies line by line, and finding hidden therein a coded message which validated, or legitimated, the existence and life of the community. It was a way of hooking in to the past, not of writing quite new works for the future.

The method grew, in fact, out of three basic and strongly held Jewish beliefs of the period. These were the beliefs (a) that Israel's God would restore his people, i.e. bring them back from exile; (b) that this hadn't happened yet, despite the geographical return from Babylon; (c) that when this happened it would be 'according to the scriptures', i.e. in fulfilment of the prophetic writings of the Hebrew Bible. Since the Essene community

believed that the real 'return from exile' was starting to happen
with their own community, it was natural that they should find
ways of asserting that the prophets had 'really' been talking
about them.

But if this was the rationale for the 'pesher' method in the
first place, there is no reason whatever to suppose that it was
then put to a totally new use, as Thiering thinks it was, in the
form of writing new 'coded' documents for other people in turn
to unscramble. 'Pesher' was a way of saying 'we are the people
spoken of by the prophets', not 'we are the people who can set
new crossword puzzles for others to solve'.

What is more, the actual 'pesher' documents that we possess
signal their existence by the use of the word *pesher* itself in
almost every other line. I have a photograph of columns 3–6 of
the Qumran Habakkuk Commentary on my study wall as I write.
The word *pesher* occurs about a dozen times in these four
columns. It is almost always preceded by a small gap in the text,
indicating that the scribe is aware, and wants his readers to be
aware, that he is 'decoding' as he goes along. *There is nothing in
the writing of actual 'pesher'-style works which corresponds in any
way to what we find in the gospels.* This conclusion, which should
be obvious to anyone who has studied the Scrolls which use
'pesher' exegesis, is fatal to Thiering's whole enterprise.

Imagery in the Gospels

This is not to say, of course, that the gospels do not use multi-
layered imagery. But this is regularly of two sorts, neither of
which corresponds to what Thiering misleadingly calls 'pesher'.

First, there is 'apocalyptic', that is, the use of cosmic imagery
(sun, moon, stars, etc.) to invest major events within the space-
time world with their theological significance. This can indeed
function like a sort of 'code'. Thus, in Daniel 7, the four 'beasts'
who come up out of the 'sea' stand for evil empires which are
attacking the people of God. The 'Son of Man' stands for the
'people of the saints of the Most High' who will be vindicated
after their suffering. Here there is, if you like, a kind of 'code'.
What does Thiering do with it? She treats it as if it were a literal
prediction (p. 154).

Second, there are the parables. These are not merely 'earthly
stories with heavenly meanings'; they are often coded retellings
of Israel's story. A good example is the parable of the Wicked
Tenants (Mark 12.1–12), which takes up a theme from Isaiah 5
and develops it in relation to the Israel of Jesus' day. Here,
again, there is something of a 'code'. But in Thiering's hands the
parables take on a new and bizarre lease of life. They are a
detailed code for the history of the community, with (for
instance) 'Lazarus' in the parable of the Rich Man and Lazarus
(Luke 16.19–31) being an actual historical person, who is
situated in a place, within the geography of Qumran itself, which
is called, again in code, 'Abraham's bosom' (p. 121f.).

Thiering's reading of genuine imagery, then, does not inspire
confidence in her ability to alert us to the presence of a different
kind of imagery altogether. Confidence decreases still further
when we see what she does in practice with her so-called
'pesher' method. Basically, she uses it when it suits her, and
ignores it at other times. Having said that accounts of
'supernatural' events are code for events in the life of the community, it is very odd that she doesn't apply this to the greatest
'supernatural' event of all – Jesus' death and resurrection.
Granted her own method, this ought to have been 'code' for
Jesus' demotion within the community and then his promotion
to high office once more. Instead, she resorts to a laughably
incredible retelling of the story.

Places and People

Thiering's geographical 'code' is actually farcical. The place-
names in the gospels, she says, are mostly code for small areas
within the Qumran settlement. The 'Mount of Olives', for
instance, isn't the hill of that name immediately to the east of
Jerusalem. It turns out to be 'code' for the house at Qumran
where celibates live. Even 'heaven' and 'earth' become the
names of places and/or parts of buildings. When Jesus is
'carried up into heaven', this means 'that he was taken up to the
raised platform in the vestry, used by the priests for their
prayers' (p. 127).

What Thiering does with the people in the story is even more
incredible. Most of the central characters turn out to have

numerous alternative names or designations, so that persons
who seem on the surface of the text to be quite distinct from one
another turn out to be one and the same all along. This is at the
heart of the detailed outworking of Thiering's argument, not
least in relation to Jesus' supposed family life.

Thus Mary, Jesus' mother, is the same person as Dorcas the
widow in Acts 9. John Mark is also the Beloved Disciple. That
might be enough of a problem for most scholars, but Thiering
goes on to identify him with, on the one hand, the centurion at
the foot of the cross (Mark 15.39), and, on the other, the
Eutychus who fell out of a window when Paul was preaching
(Acts 20.7–12), and who was then restored to life (this is code, of
course, for John Mark's demotion and re-promotion in the community). Mary Magdalene is identified with 'Jairus' daughter'
(her 'raising' indicates, once more, promotion in the community); she is then also identified with the maid named Rhoda
in Acts 12, which enables Thiering to mount her argument about
Jesus' divorce, on the basis that Rhoda is called 'mad'.

This would be enough to make most readers say that, if there
is madness here, it is not that of Rhoda. But there is more. The
word 'crowds' does not refer to crowds, but to the Jewish king
Agrippa I. The word 'all' does not mean 'all', but is a code for
whichever king of the Herod dynasty was ruling at the time. The
word 'earthquake' is a title which was used by both Theudas and
Apollos. The word 'Pharisees' denotes the Chief Priest,
Caiaphas. Again one asks: are we so sure that this is not simply
an elaborate hoax?

Perhaps the most fantastic of these multiple identities is
Simon Magus, who according to Thiering is 'the main character
apart from Jesus' in the whole story (p. 395). He turns out to be
the same person as Simon 'the Leper' (i.e. outcast, at one stage,
from the community);[6] as 'Lazarus' who is 'raised from the dead'
in John 11, and also the Lazarus who is located in 'Abraham's
bosom' in Luke 16; as 'Ananias'; and as one of the two 'thieves'
crucified along with Jesus, who, despite having both legs broken,
administers an antidote to Jesus' poison drug while both of them
are in the cave after being crucified.

The net effect of all this fantastic name-swapping is rather
like the effect you get if you try to stage a Shakespeare play with
a cast of five actors. The same people keep reappearing in dif-

ferent identities. If the audience get confused, that's just too bad.
Thiering's readers may well feel the same way.

Jesus' Family?

What is the evidence for Thiering's sensationalist claim, that
Jesus married Mary Magdalene, had a daughter and two sons,
then divorced her and married Lydia? What weight, if any, can
be put on it?

The evidence for marriage to Mary comes in the *Gospel of
Philip*. This, according to one reputable modern edition, was
written in the second half of the third century AD.[7] That puts it
as long after Jesus' life as we are, today, after the time of
George the Second, when Handel and Bach were writing music
and George Washington was a small boy. The same edition comments that 'the line of thought is often rambling and disjointed';
it tells us a good deal about third-century practice in the gnostic
sect which wrote it, but nothing of any value about the first
century.

The passage about Jesus and Mary Magdalene is sandwiched
between snippets whose flavour may be gleaned from the following:

> God is a man-eater. For this reason men are sacrificed to
> him. Before men were sacrificed animals were being
> sacrificed, since those to whom they were sacrificed were not
> gods.

> The Lord went into the dye works of Levi. He took seventy-
> two different colours and threw them into the vat. He took
> them out all white. And he said, 'Even so has the Son of Man
> come as a dyer.'

> As for the unclean spirits, there are males among them and
> there are females. The males are they which unite with the
> souls which inhabit a female form, but the females are they
> which are mingled with those in a male form, through one
> who was disobedient.

One is bound to ask, would we trust a document like this to give us accurate information about events that had happened two hundred and fifty years before? Yet this is the context in which we find Thiering's crucial passage. In the *Gospel of Philip*, columns 63 and 64, we read:

> The companion of the Savior is Mary Magdalene. But Christ loved her more than all the disciples and used to kiss her often on the mouth. The rest of the disciples were offended by it and expressed disapproval. They said to him, 'Why do you love her more than all of us?' The Savior answered and said to them, 'Why do I not love you like her?' When a blind man and one who sees are both together in darkness, they are no different from one another. When the light comes, then he who sees will see the light, and he who is blind will remain in darkness.[8]

This, frankly, tells us a good deal about the tortuous gnostic speculations of the third century. It gives us no information whatsoever about the real Jesus or the real Mary Magdalene.

Discovering Thiering's evidence for saying that Jesus had a daughter is somewhat difficult. On p. 128 she says that a daughter had been born, and gives a footnote to support this. In the note, we are directed to the chronological chart on p. 251. There it simply says that 'a daughter had just been born'. No other evidence is offered; no coded passage in the gospels or Acts. Just a simple assertion.

Most readers will feel that her evidence for the two subsequent children, both boys, is equally thin. According to Acts 6.7, 'the Word of God increased'. Jesus, of course, is the 'word of God', as in John 1.1–14; so the phrase means that Jesus' family grew larger (p. 133). When the phrase occurs again in Acts 12.24 it means the same thing: another son was born (p. 141). This is simply an exegetical circus stunt.

The divorce rests on similarly flimsy evidence (actually, calling it 'evidence' at all gives it a status which it doesn't deserve). The crucial discussion is on pp. 146–7. Mary Magdalene is identified, as we saw, with Rhoda in Acts 12. The disciples told her she was 'mad'; this means, apparently, that she belonged to an ecstatic order which was associated with zealotry, so that 'she could no longer be counted with Christians'. She was thus an 'unbeliever', and so (according to Paul in 1 Corinthians 7) could be divorced.

Jesus then married Lydia (a female bishop, by the way), as we 'know' from the fact that, in Acts 16.14, we read that 'A certain woman named Lydia, a worshipper of God, was listening to us; she was from the city of Thyatira and a dealer in purple cloth. The Lord opened her heart to listen eagerly to what was said by Paul.' This, according to Thiering, means that 'the Lord opened her heart' in the sense that Jesus and Lydia fell in love and got married. For some reason the same phrase indicates, according to Thiering, that Lydia was, until that point, a virgin.

This is 'confirmed', says Thiering, by a very obscure passage from the Scroll called the Damascus Document, at the foot of column 4 and the top of column 5. This describes a dispute over people who take extra wives.[9] It is exactly the sort of thing we might expect to find in an Essene document waging a war of words against a rival Jewish group. It tells us nothing whatsoever about Jesus of Nazareth, or indeed anyone else in the first century AD.

These 'arguments' are so amazingly thin that it is hard even to know how to answer them. If texts can mean this, they can mean quite literally anything. Thiering is right to say that her theory about Jesus' 'family' is not at the centre of her work. But let us be clear: it is this passage in the book, and this alone, which has raised her status from a writer of complex, obscure and unconvincing theories to that of worldwide bestseller. And the passage in question consists of just this: a few pages of totally worthless argument.

Death and Resurrection

We have already observed the oddity that Thiering does not treat the stories of Jesus' crucifixion and resurrection as another example of a coded statement about demotion and promotion within the community. She tries, instead, to give a 'historical' account of 'what actually happened' which involves an actual crucifixion and an actual 'rising'. The crucifixion, she says, did not result in Jesus' death; the 'rising' was effected by a medical antidote to the drug which had caused Jesus to swoon on the cross. Leaving that aside, there are several other things which make one think, frankly, that believing the accounts in the gospels is child's play compared with believing Thiering's reconstruction.

For a start, there is the extraordinary theory that Pontius Pilate, the Roman governor, was sent for by the sect, and came down to the Dead Sea to supervise Jesus' crucifixion in person. This is totally absurd. (It is on a level, though, with some of Thiering's other ideas, such as that of people being baptized in the Dead Sea: this suggests that she has not herself tried totally immersing herself in that noxious and buoyant water.) All our evidence suggests that crucifixion was a punishment meted out by Romans on subject peoples, not, as in Thiering's reconstruction, something done by one part of a Jewish sect to another, with the Roman governor coming in alongside.[10]

Then there is the extraordinary idea that the two other men crucified with Jesus (Judas Iscariot and Simon Magus) could have had their legs broken and still have survived – survived, indeed, so well that Simon Magus could act as doctor for Jesus in the cave into which they were placed. When crucified people had their legs broken, they died very quickly, from asphyxiation. A crucified person stayed alive on a cross by using his legs to force his body upwards and so make breathing possible. Once the legs were broken, that was impossible. Here again one wonders at the arbitrary way in which Thiering applies, or does not apply, her 'code'. Could not 'breaking the legs' have been a 'pesher' for an attempt to demote someone in the community?

As with many speculative theories about Jesus, it is Thiering's attempts to deal with the resurrection which show just how thin the whole thing really is. She begins with the extraordinary statement that the idea of Jesus' resurrection has only recently become central in Christianity, and that in the first generation it was merely an incidental belief. It has only really caught on as a central idea, according to Thiering, in the last two hundred years or so (p. 118), as part of a fundamentalist quest for solid facts as the basis for faith.

This is one of the most extraordinary statements in this bizarre book. Our earliest Christian documents, the writings of Paul, are full of belief in Jesus' resurrection. When Paul says 'if Christ is not raised, your faith is worthless' (1 Corinthians 15.17), this does not amount to saying, as Thiering suggests, 'If these facts are not right, then I am going to be very upset' (p. 117).

They mean that the whole reason for Christianity to exist depends on the fact that Jesus is alive again. If he simply died on a Roman cross as a messianic pretender, that would have marked him out, for Paul, as yet another deluded fanatic who led Israel astray. This needs to be stressed most emphatically: there was no reason whatever for Paul to follow, preach about, or celebrate a Jesus who had simply been crucified. Lots of others people were crucified in the first century. Nobody ever hailed them subsequently as the living Lord.

In addition, Thiering ignores what Paul actually says. The line about 'faith being in vain, unless Christ is raised' comes midway through a long argument. At the very beginning of the passage, however, Paul emphasizes again and again that Jesus was seen, alive, by one person, then another, then another, including at one point by 'five hundred brothers and sisters at one time, most of whom are still alive, although some have died' (1 Corinthians 15.6). This is not a rhetorical statement that one will be upset if things don't seem to be this way after all. This is an appeal to evidence, evidence that his hearers could in principle check for themselves.

It is totally absurd to say that Christianity from then on didn't make the resurrection of Jesus central. The exact opposite is the case. So much so, in fact, that (as all scholars know) one of the difficult things in reading the gospels is to sort out the difference between (a) what happened at the time and (b) the glow which is cast over all the events by the writers' belief that Jesus is alive again, and present with them. As we move forward through church history, it is impossible to marginalize the resurrection. Writer after writer emphasizes it. To suggest that it only became important in the last two centuries is to betray a shocking lack of knowledge of the entire Christian tradition. Thiering cites one or two late gnostic texts as evidence for some people thinking that Jesus hadn't really died on the cross. These prove nothing at all, except that later gnosticism, like later Islam, had a hard time fitting the real Jesus into its worldview.

I shall say more about the resurrection of Jesus in the next chapter. For the moment it is enough to say that Thiering's great edifice is based on thin air, built of imaginary bricks, and topped off with a non-existent roof. It is not even a house of cards. It is not a house at all.

What's Left?

What is left of Thiering's theory, then? Not much. Her appeal to the idea of a jigsaw puzzle looks more and more suspicious. She has put together the historical puzzle of Jesus and early Christianity by the dubious method of re-cutting all the bits of the puzzle so that they fit each other despite their original shape. Where this still doesn't work, she has decided, quite arbitrarily, that the two bits of picture she is trying to fit together are 'really' the same. If one jigsaw piece has a horse on it, and the next one a rabbit, the naive puzzle-solver will think they don't match. Thiering simply announces that, in the 'pesher' method, horses and rabbits are the same thing. John Mark is the centurion at the foot of the cross. Mary Magdalene is Jairus' daughter, and also the maid, Rhoda. Anyone can do jigsaw puzzles by this method. It's like someone trying to solve a Rubik's cube by peeling off the coloured stickers and arranging them neatly together, side by side, without ever wrestling with the cube itself at all.

In short, if Thiering's book were a play, or a movie, or even an opera, the audience would have become impatient long before the end. We are prepared to suspend disbelief a certain amount, but not that much. Believing that Jesus was more or less as the gospels say he was may be quite difficult for people who live in a very different world. As we have seen, however, several world-class scholars have been putting the historical jigsaw together in ways that vindicate large parts of the gospels, without recourse to the fantastic speculations of a Thiering. But believing in Thiering's Jesus asks too much of us. If we can believe that, we can believe anything.

What is it about the Essenes that inclines some people to look to them for historical inspiration? By all accounts (other than Thiering's), they were a small group. Their significance for us as historians lies not least in the fact that, by sheer historical accident, we happen to have first-hand documentation of their communal life and beliefs. They enable us to sink a shaft at one small point into the worldview which some Jews held at the time. But Thiering is not the only one to find in them a bizarre inspiration for work on Jesus.

As I was drafting this chapter, a friend lent me another new book, called *Jesus and the Essenes*.[11] In this, the author describes a series of interviews with someone who, under hypnosis,

'regressed' into a series of previous lives. This eventually
enabled her, in turn, to 'interview' a member of the Essene community. And this Essene, obligingly enough, told her about Jesus
. . . When I wrote above that Thiering's book was one of the
most bizarre I had ever read, I hadn't bargained for this. Somehow, the combination of Essenism, reincarnation, astrology,
secret information, and Jesus becomes irresistible. Are we
moving, as a society, towards a new period of esoteric, gnostic-
style speculation?

Thiering herself seems to think that some form of Christianity
can still survive, despite all her ideas. Indeed, she seems to think
that some radical revision like this is necessary. When she and I
appeared together on television, she justified her ideas by saying
she was taking the 'male icon' away from Christianity by making
Jesus just an ordinary man. And she justified this, in turn, by
saying that the key thing about the Reformation in the sixteenth
century was that it removed the 'female icon' of the Virgin Mary.
(Here, again, her understanding of church history seems to leave
a good deal to be desired.)

Her own emphases, not least her highlighting of Simon
Magus, make one wonder where we might end up if we followed
her lead. As she ends the chapter on Jesus' divorce, she discusses the church's attempts to hold together Jesus' humanity
and divinity. 'It may be,' she writes, 'following the urgings of our
own time, that the divinity has to be sacrificed to the humanity.'
Even those who are themselves faced with complex moral
dilemmas may not feel that the 'urgings of our own time' are an
entirely satisfactory basis upon which to build a theology or a
religion. One is left with the impression that Thiering's whole
theory has grown out of just such 'urgings'. Very well: but let us
not mistake it, at any point, for history.

And history, after all, is what Christianity is all about. This
leads us away from the lush, lurid world of Thiering's speculations, and towards the cooler, drier world of scepticism
inhabited by A. N. Wilson.

3

A. N. Wilson: A Moderately Pale Galilean

The Simple Jesus?

It must have been somewhat galling for Barbara Thiering and
A. N. Wilson when each discovered that the other was about to
publish a much-heralded new book on Jesus. It's rather like
planning a surprise arrival at a party, dressed as Father
Christmas, only to discover that someone else has had the same
idea. Children at the party will be suspicious. They can't *both* be
the real Father Christmas . . . which leads to the nasty suspicion
that perhaps *neither* of them is.

Wilson and Thiering, of course, don't believe in Father
Christmas. They don't actually believe in Christmas itself, or not
very much. Thiering, as we have just seen, believes in a Jesus
whose life was bounded by the strange organization and counter-
organization of a marginal Palestinian sect. What sort of Jesus
does Wilson believe in?

Wilson – who in real life is a novelist, journalist, and prize-
winning writer of biographies – comes out of his corner fighting.
He recently wrote a little book attacking all 'religion', making it
clear that, though he had been a practising Christian for most of
his life, he has now emphatically given all that up.[1] Now he
roundly declares that Jesus himself wouldn't have approved of
Christianity either.[2]

The real, historical Jesus, he claims, has nothing to do with
the Christ-figure of Christianity, or the church, or the Eucharist.
These, he says, are 'myth'. (I started to count the number of
times he said 'myth' in the television documentary on 22 September, but I couldn't keep up.) Strip off the layers of colourful
dogma and imagery, get back to the real historical Jesus . . . and
what you'll find is a simple Galilean holy man who would have
been horrified at what is now done in his name. Wilson's book
ends starkly: if Jesus 'had foreseen the whole of Christian his-

tory, his despair would have been even greater' than it was when
he cried out 'My God, why hast thou forsaken me?' He might
have wished he had never been born.

Wilson prepares the way for his main argument with two
preliminary moves. First, there is Paul – who, Wilson, thinks,
was the real inventor of 'Christianity' as we know it. He was
muddled and self-contradictory. He took the Jewish message of
Jesus, and totally distorted it into a pagan-style religion, with
Jesus as a pagan-style divine figure. He turned Jesus' simple
meal with his followers into the Christian Eucharist. He took
Jesus' Jewish vision of an inner Kingdom of the soul and made it
into a worldwide missionary organization. Perhaps worst of all,
he cast his influence so heavily over the writers of at least three
of the gospels – Matthew, Mark and Luke – that they then retold
the story of Jesus in such a way as to embody his (Paul's) ideas,
giving subsequent generations the misguided impression that
Jesus was actually like the Christ-figure that Paul himself had
invented.

This leads to the second preliminary point. The gospels, Wilson roundly asserts, are not unbiased accounts, 'dispassionate'
history. They are thoroughly prejudiced Christian propaganda-
documents. They invent fictitious stories about 'Jesus', based
either on their dubious theology (which, he says, they learned
from Paul) or on their discovery of passages in the Old Testament which they thought Jesus 'must' have fulfilled. They are
thus severely distorted, and we can't trust them for sober history.
We must therefore go back behind them to rediscover the real
Jesus behind the Christ of their myth-making faith.

This clears the way for Wilson to reconstruct his own would-
be 'dispassionate' account of Jesus. Drawing particularly on the
work of my Oxford colleague, the highly distinguished Jewish
historian Geza Vermes, Wilson suggests that Jesus was basically
a Galilean *hasid*, a holy man.[3] He didn't think he was the Messiah; still less did he think he was the Second Person of the
Trinity. He was born in the ordinary way, and pretty certainly in
Nazareth, not Bethlehem. He taught an inner morality, an
'indestructible inner kingdom' (p. 163). He tried to raise the
status of women, and lower the nationalist ambitions of men. He
symbolically opposed the Jerusalem Temple, warning that if the
Jews were not careful their precious national system would all
come tumbling down.

But when push came to shove, his message failed to make sense (p. 177). His followers deserted him, and the Romans, suspicious of the messianic pretensions which the crowds had wished upon him, executed him. He stayed dead; his disciples most likely took his body back to Galilee for burial there. After his death, however, his brother, James, reassured his followers that all had happened 'according to the scriptures'. Due to family likeness and general confusion, he was mistaken for Jesus, and the story got around that Jesus himself had been raised from the dead. Then, a little while later, Paul invented a new religion based loosely on the idea, rather than the actual life, of Jesus; and the rest is . . . church history.

Glimpses of Truth

Wilson allows that the gospels, though biased, may contain some truth. 'Having admitted', he says, 'that the Gospel-narratives must be treated with circumspection . . . , it would be careless to dismiss them altogether' (p. 210). It is only right to accord Wilson himself the same benefit of the doubt. If, as we shall see, we are bound to disagree with a good deal of his book, this does not mean that he has missed the point entirely. What is there here that a serious historian can affirm? What is there, even, that a Christian can welcome?

It was a great advance to recognize that the gospels were written *from a point of view*. This insight, however, is not Wilson's. As we saw in the first chapter, it has been a commonplace of New Testament study for at least a century. This actually sets us free from a good many things that otherwise get in the way, such as the absurd calculation that used to go on of just how often the cock crowed during Jesus' trial. (Each of the gospel writers tells the story in a different way, and if you're not careful you end up harmonizing them by saying that the cock crowed nine times . . . which none of the gospels say!) Once we accept that the evangelists all wrote the story in their own way, we can escape that sort of nonsense for ever and get on with the real job.

So, too, it was a great advance to recognize that Jesus belongs firmly in the world of first-century Judaism. This, too, is an insight which the church itself has never entirely lost, even though it has often tried to do so, and which has been firmly restored by the scholarship of the last twenty years in particular. When Geza Vermes published his book *Jesus the Jew* in 1973, the title itself caused something of a *frisson*: Jesus was really a *Jew*? The fact that today the phrase sounds commonplace is just one of several great debts that we owe to Vermes (along with his pioneering work on the Dead Sea Scrolls). Wilson is right to pick this up and make it his starting-point.

In particular, I think Wilson has his finger on something when he discusses, in his eighth, ninth and tenth chapters, Jesus' attitude towards the Jewish system of his day, and his beliefs about his impending death. We need to look at this a little more closely.

On p. 187 he writes that 'Jesus might actually have foreseen, forty years before it happened, that the Jewish race would suffer the most terrible overthrow at the hands of the Romans.' This, as we saw, is an insight emphasized by Marcus Borg. Wilson then suggests that Jesus wanted his contemporaries to embrace 'a simple Judaism, stripped of its besetting sins of moralism and sectarianism'. Only so, he believed, could the Kingdom come. There I think the emphasis is significantly out of line, but at least the starting-point is right. His treatment of Jesus in Gethsemane (pp. 199–203) is moving, and full of insight. Taken together, these two points lead to the fine statement (p. 219f.): 'With tragic irony, we can see that Jesus was never more truly the representative of his race than when he was being tortured and killed.' Wilson thinks that Jesus himself foresaw his own death, and gave it this kind of interpretation (p. 178f.). I shall return to this in my final chapter.

How are we to look at all this? Sometimes, when using modern roads, one finds oneself driving parallel to the road one wishes to be on, but unable to get to it because of a hedge in the way. At points like these in his book I have a sense that Wilson is running on a line parallel to the actual truth, and not very far away. The hedge between the two roads may be quite thin in parts, and there may yet be light visible through it.

Getting to Grips with the Detail

History, like music, has to get the details right. It is all very well to say, with the famous conductor Sir Thomas Beecham, that, as long as the orchestra starts together and finishes together, what happens in between doesn't matter very much. The conductor may have a grand scheme for the overall flow of the music, but any discerning listener will soon tell whether the individual instrumentalists are in fact playing in tune and keeping time. Wilson's historical hypothesis, like a symphony concert heard from outside the hall, sounds interesting and at times quite impressive. What happens when we go into the hall and listen more closely?

Scholarship

Wilson professes to have studied the subject very seriously. His publishers describe the book as 'scholarly'. The fact that it has lots of footnotes, and a large bibliography, gives the casual reader the impression that the details have all been carefully nailed down in their proper place.

I have to say that this appearance is deceptive. Wilson has clearly read some of the recent scholarly writing about Jesus; equally, there is a lot (including much that is in his bibliography) whose impact is nowhere to be seen. There has been, as we saw, a very great deal of writing about Jesus in the last couple of decades, much of it very serious and very helpful. Wilson has not taken more than a small fraction of it on board. (There is a wonderfully patronizing footnote on p. 127: Wilson says that Sanders' book *Jesus and Judaism* 'has many valuable insights into Jesus' relationship with contemporary Judaism'. This sounds like a ten-year old choirboy complimenting Dame Kiri te Kanawa on having sung really quite prettily.) There are several questions that must be raised briefly, before we can get to the heart of the matter.

First, most of Wilson's strongest points are not his own, but are taken from bits and pieces of the scholarship of the last hundred years. This is not of course to say that they are wrong, only that they do not have the novelty value that one might imagine from the publicity surrounding the book.

Second, he uses the word 'myth' to mean simply 'untruth', which has been shown again and again to be thoroughly misleading. Until a more nuanced account of how 'myth' works is introduced, the category is always going to be misleading.

Third, Wilson's view of Paul belongs to an era of Pauline studies now long past. It's a pity he didn't at least read Sanders' book *Paul and Palestinian Judaism* as well as his *Jesus and Judaism*; that might have saved him from some of his more bizarre remarks about the apostle, which reflect a way of reading Paul now almost entirely discredited.[4] And as for his theory that Paul was the same person as the 'Malchus' who had his ear cut off in the Garden of Gethsemane (pp. 27, 204–6) . . . that is an idea worthy of Barbara Thiering herself.

Fourth, Wilson tries to hold several incompatible theories about John's gospel at the same time. It is serious history, as John Robinson said (p. 49). It is fictitious, designed to go with the Jewish lectionary, as Aileen Guilding said (p. 50). It is a potentially gnostic book (p. 54). It has echoes of the Dead Sea Scrolls (p. 54). It is anti-Pauline (p. 55). How do we know where we are in all this?

These things all cause problems, but do not necessarily spell complete disaster. In addition, however, at point after point Wilson fails to take care of the scholarly pence; so how can we be sure that the pounds are looking after themselves?

Details of Palestinian History

A few examples, taken almost at random. Many of them concern the Jewish context of Jesus' ministry; this is, after all, just the thing that a 'dispassionate historian' should get right. Wilson doesn't know Palestinian geography very well: he says (p. 116) that John the Baptist was imprisoned in the north of the country, whereas in fact, as Josephus makes clear, the prison was in Herod's fort Machaerus, in the segment of Herod's territory that came down the east side of the Jordan, to a point in the south of the country near the Dead Sea, roughly opposite Qumran. On p. 99 Wilson accepts at face value Josephus' statement, that Galilee was a hotbed of revolution; whereas the Irish scholar Sean Freyne, whom Wilson interviewed on his television documentary, has demonstrated in his book *Galilee from Alexander the Great to Hadrian: 323 B.C.E. to 135 C.E.*[5] that this was not the case. Josephus was shooting a line; Wilson has accepted it uncritically. Wilson also misconceives the relationships between the 'Zealots' and the 'Sicarii' (pp. 100, 128); and he misunderstands the rabbinic debate about sowing and ploughing (p. 122). None of this encourages us to trust him as a historian of first-century Palestine.

Dotting the 'i's

In addition, Wilson gets a sufficient number of references wrong to give one the impression that his homework was done in something of a hurry. Two or three examples must suffice.

Anyone looking up Mark 3.3 to check on the statement that Jews had to keep the Passover inside the walls of Jerusalem or face a heavy beating (p. 191) would be puzzled, since Mark 3.3 says nothing about the matter.[6] Eventually light dawns: the reference is to *Makk.* 3.3, where 'Makk.' stands for the Rabbinic tractate 'Makkoth'. This is part of the 'Mishnah', the codification of Jewish law. No doubt this is a mere typographical error, though a very confusing one. It raises, however, further problems: the Mishnah wasn't compiled until 200 years after Jesus' day. It is virtually certain that much of its legislation is idealized, and doesn't represent the way things were before the destruction of the Temple in AD 70. It is highly unlikely that the authorities would have allowed zealous rabbis to inflict ritual beatings on persons who, in the thronging festival crowds, decided to eat their passover meal outside the city walls.

This mistake goes with another. On p. 123 Wilson says that Jesus probably got his ideas about the mustard-seed from reading law-books, namely the Palestinian Talmud. Problem: the Talmud is basically a commentary on the Mishnah, which was itself (as we just noted) written in about AD 200. The Talmud itself wasn't written down until about *AD 400*. If Wilson is worried about the Jesus of history not being able to do the extraordinary things credited to him by Christianity, I think we are entitled to ask Wilson whether his historical Jesus was capable of reading a book written four hundred years after his own day. It is like suggesting that Shakespeare got his ideas from Tom Stoppard.

There is more. Jerusalem, says Wilson (p. 191f.), is extremely cold at Passover time. He cites Mark 13.24, 25. That text is all about the sun and the moon being darkened, and the stars falling from heaven . . . surely Wilson doesn't think this is a literal description of a bitter Jerusalem evening at Passover-time? All right, Simon Peter did warm himself at a charcoal fire (Mark 14.54). But in Jerusalem, in April, Spring is already quite well advanced. It can get on the chilly side at night (I once caught a cold there by sitting out of doors at a café on an April evening), but there would be no problem about pilgrims camping out of doors, perhaps with small fires to keep warm. Or again, Wilson gets references to Josephus wrong, putting the story of John the Baptist in *Antiquities* 17 instead of 18 (p. 114). A slip of the pen, no doubt; but it seems harsh when he then says (p. 124) that Josephus himself is 'notoriously inaccurate with statistics'. He says that Paul's Letter to the Romans makes no reference to the cross of Jesus, whereas in fact the letter is about little else (surely he can't simply mean that the word 'cross' itself is absent?). He has John the Baptist clothed in goatskins (pp. 102, 109), whereas the text clearly says camelskins. And, as various reviewers have pointed out, he says emphatically (p. 123) that there is no mention of colour in the gospels – only then to refer, later, to Jesus wearing a purple cloak (p. 211).

None of this, frankly, gives us any confidence in Wilson's ability to look after the details of his own dispassionate history-writing. As long as we stay outside the concert-hall, the music sounds interesting and daring; when we come inside, we are able to hear that several of the instruments are playing quite badly out of tune.

'Dispassionate History'?

Wilson sets out with a grand claim: his book 'aims to be a dispassionate account of Jesus' (p. xvi). To write in this way, he says, means that one must 'empty the mind and take nothing for granted' (p. 8). This, I suggest, is a 'myth' in two senses. First, it corresponds to nothing in reality (as Wilson himself, in a moment of candour, more or less concedes on p. 75). Second, it is a story told by a community to legitimate its own existence. What is this community? It is the Western culture of the last two hundred years, which has tried to separate out 'facts' from 'values', or 'events' from 'interpretations' ('memory which made no interpretation of facts', as Wilson says on p. 53). This is the myth of 'objectivity', the idea of the 'neutral' observer who is a mere fly on the wall, perceiving things with almost a God's-eye view. It is this idea that has enabled Wilson to claim that, whereas Christians are looking at things with faith-tinted spectacles, he is simply studying the facts, straight.

'Straight Facts'?

In my youth it was notorious that the newspaper which claimed to 'give you the facts, straight' was the old *Morning Star* – the official organ of the Communist Party of Great Britain. This taught me, and I'm surprised it didn't teach Wilson, to be suspicious of people who claim to be unprejudiced, impartial observers or historians. Anthropologists have often discovered that native peoples behave differently, when being watched by an anthropologist, from how they behave when all by themselves. Historians have started to realize the same point, too: when we ask questions about the past they remain precisely *our* questions. We do not see the past from a 'neutral' perspective.

Actually, Wilson's publishers blew the gaff on this point (which is central to the whole book) when they printed on the dust-jacket a single line from the *Daily Telegraph* review of one of Wilson's earlier, and justly famous, books, his biography of C. S. Lewis. Lewis, of course, was, like Wilson himself, a brilliant literary critic, and Wilson makes due acknowledgment of that fact. Lewis was also a very popular Christian apologist, and Wilson, as a would-be anti-Christian apologist, tears him to shreds on that score. Wilson, of course, as a good modern writer, was just looking at things objectively, telling the facts as one should . . .

If you believe that, you'll believe anything. The *Telegraph* review of the Lewis biography says it all, pulling the rug out from under Wilson's *Jesus* as it does so: 'Passionate, perspicacious, funny and inevitably partisan.' That, of course, is why it's such a good book; but, note, it's *passionate*, not 'dispassionate', and it's *partisan*. Wilson clearly takes sides, *as all writers inevitably do*. There's the rub. Actually, I think Wilson's verdict on Lewis applies nicely to Wilson himself: excellent on literary criticism, but don't trust him when it comes to theology.

The Historian and 'Bias'

Even supposing such a thing as dispassionate history about Jesus were possible, is Wilson the man to give it to us? Well, what would qualify someone for the task? That's not an easy question, but I know what certainly *dis*qualifies someone. If you want a dispassionate account of the Gulf War, don't ask Saddam Hussein or Norman Schwarzkopf. If you want a dispassionate account of Jesus, don't ask someone who has recently published a rampaging and swashbuckling root-and-branch attack on all religion.

Wilson constantly implies that regular historians (on p. 61 he cites the Roman writers Tacitus and Livy) wrote things 'straight', whereas the gospel writers, of course, told them at a slant. Has he *read* Tacitus or Livy recently? Tacitus, though he claims to write without bias, flaunts his hatred of the Roman emperors on every other page. Livy, by contrast, tells the story of Rome so as to lead the eye up to the great achievements of his patron, Augustus. Very convenient. Very typical of all history.

The fact is (!) that you can't write about anything from a 'neutral' point of view. There is no such thing. Every telling of every event involves selection; and when you select you interpret. I choose to tell my wife about some things that I've done today, not (I hope) because I want to hide other things, but because she really doesn't need to hear about every time I took a breath, every time I opened and shut my study door, every time I looked out of the window. I select the less usual, the less humdrum, the less predictable events, and arrange them into brief narratives. That, of course, imposes my point of view on things. Not to do so would be impossible. Even to attempt not to do so would be impossibly tedious.

Literary Allusions

In particular, all such selection, at whatever level, takes place in a *context*. I am the person that I have become through a myriad of large and small influences, some of them landmarks in our culture (the Bible, Shakespeare, Handel, Bach, Beethoven, Sibelius, George Herbert, T. S. Eliot, Gerard Manley Hopkins, if you want to know). If, in the course of my conversation with my wife, I allude deliberately or accidentally to some or all of the above, does this mean I am necessarily making up what I am saying to fit some literary convention, some plot in which (as in David Lodge's brilliant novel *The British Museum is Falling Down*) 'life' suddenly starts to imitate 'Art'? Of course not.

We should not, then, be surprised if the gospel writers tell stories in such a way as to echo the Old Testament. Nor should we assume (as Wilson does on p. 52 and elsewhere) that when this happens they are simply writing pious fiction. He constantly suggests that where we find an incident in the gospels which echoes or mirrors something in the Old Testament, this is an indication that the writer is standing in a literary tradition which has imposed its ideas upon him to such an extent that he has turned it into 'history'. The gospel writers, according to this model, invented 'incidents' that didn't happen, in order simply to fit something in the earlier tradition.

Wilson himself, of course, also stands within a literary tradition. As a good writer will, he quotes, or alludes to, Shakespeare, Tolstoy and many others. When he says that John Robinson intended 'to give us pause' (p. 59) he is quoting from *Hamlet*, Act Three. When he talks of the believer 'bobbing about in the sea of faith' (p. 66) he is quoting Matthew Arnold (or perhaps Don Cupitt). He explains John's telling of the 'whopping lie' of the resurrection story (p. 66f.) by referring to William Blake, who, though a good and charming man in his own way, had a funny habit of claiming to have conversed with angels. And so on. This doesn't of itself invalidate what he says. It's merely how good writers often write. I think he is correct about John Robinson, and wrong about the Fourth Gospel, but I reach those judgments on grounds unrelated to the presence of literary allusion.

To test the truth of his assertions we must look elsewhere, namely, to the actual evidence. There, unfortunately for Wilson, things run against him. His odd remark about there being no mention of colour in the gospels (p. 123) is something he says he picked up from André Gide. In other words, he made up a manifest and blatant untruth about the gospels, in order to fit in with something in his literary tradition. The point for the historian, then, is not whether there is a literary, or biblical, allusion present in a text. The point is whether the evidence supports what is said.

When it comes to the gospels themselves, then of course all
sensible readers see at once that they are written from a position
of Christian faith. Not to notice this is to remain at the level of
reading ability that thinks something is true 'because I read it in
the papers'. So what? Does Wilson seriously think that if we had
access to Pilate's court records they would be 'unbiased' or
'dispassionate'? Does he think that Josephus – that great first-
century Jewish historian, who wrote the history of the war with
Rome while living as a Jew in Rome on an Imperial pension – is
'neutral'? Of course not. So we must give up the myth of
neutrality, whether our own or that of any single source. Only
then can we start engaging in real history.

When we do that we will discover that the gospels make
remarkably good historical sense. This is a big claim, and we
must come at it from a number of angles, all of which can be
filled out by reference to fuller treatments than are possible
here.[7] Two features we must look at in particular are the Jewish
belief in one God, and the Jewish hope for the future. In both
areas Wilson follows a long line of scholars into the ditch of
thorough misunderstanding.

One God

The belief that there is only one God is normally called
'monotheism'. Wilson claims repeatedly (e.g. pp. xvi, 20, 135,
157, 249f., etc.) that people who hold this belief would find it
very difficult to believe that Jesus was 'the second person of the
Trinity'. He claims, therefore, like many others, that to treat
Jesus as in any sense 'divine' shows that one has moved off the
proper territory of Jewish monotheism and has embraced
instead a pagan, Gentile type of religion that would have
shocked any good Jew, such as Jesus himself or his first followers.

Jewish Belief

What are we to make of this?[8] The first and most important
thing to say is that Wilson has totally misunderstood what first-
century Jewish monotheism was all about. It was never, in the

Jewish literature of the crucial period, an analysis of the inner being of God, a kind of numerical statement about, so to speak, what God was like on the inside. It was always a polemical statement directed outwards against the pagan nations. 'The gods of the peoples are idols: YHWH [i.e. Israel's God] made the heavens' (Psalm 96.5). When Jews said they believed in the one true God, this was what they meant: that their own God was not merely a local or tribal deity, but was the God of the whole earth. This, of course, had immediate political consequences. If Israel was suffering at the hands of the pagans, her God would sooner or later redeem her. This is the basic meaning of Jewish monotheism, first-century style.

Significantly, within the Jewish literature of our period there are all sorts of signs that Jews developed ways of speaking about this one God which showed that they were not nearly so worried about the numerical analysis of God-on-the-inside as the later Rabbis were. (The Rabbis, of course, were faced with burgeoning Christianity, and developed the 'numerical analysis of God' idea partly as a way of arguing against it.) Jews spoke or wrote of God's 'Wisdom' as active in creating and sustaining the world. They wrote, movingly, of God's Law ('Torah') as an entity which had existed before the world was made, and which then acted in history, particularly in Israel's history. They spoke with reverence of God's 'Presence', his 'Shekinah', which dwelt in the Temple at Jerusalem. They spoke of his 'Word' ('Memra'), active in the world. Why did they do this?

They did it, regularly, in order to get round the problem of how to speak appropriately of the one true God who is *both* beyond the created world *and* active within it. Even when, as some scholars have argued, these 'manner-of-speaking' entities like Wisdom and Torah became regarded as virtually distinct beings, the Jews who referred to them didn't regard this as compromising their monotheism. They still believed that their God, the God of Israel, was the one true God, even while active through these various 'beings', and that all the other gods, the gods of the pagans, were mere idols. But they were holding on to the basic belief that this one God was both beyond the world and active within it.

The other problem you always face, if you declare faith in one true God, is to do with evil. Where did evil come from? What is this God doing about it? The Jews didn't have a clear answer to

the first question, but they did to the second. This God had
called Israel herself to be the means of blessing the world, of
saving the world, of bringing light to the world. That's why (they
believed) Israel came into being in the first place.

Monotheism and Early Christianity

What does all this do to our view of Jesus, of Paul and of the
early Christians? It puts it in a very different light from the one
you'd have got by reading Wilson. When he speaks of the early
Christian belief that Jesus was somehow on the 'divine' side of
the equation, what he doesn't notice is that the language used to
convey this belief *is all taken from precisely this Jewish stock*.
Jesus is the 'Word' of God. Jesus is the Wisdom through which
the world was made. Jesus is, in some senses, the new Torah.
And, in a move which has stupendous consequences, Jesus is the
true Shekinah, the true presence of the one true God, the truth
of which the Jerusalem Temple was simply a foretaste.[9]

This is one of the points at which, as I said earlier, Wilson
seems to me close to the truth but separated by a hedge. He
says, quite often, that one of the characteristic things Jesus did
was to 'admit people into the kingdom'. But what on earth does
that *mean*? It means, to be blunt, that Jesus was doing something, off his own bat, that normally happened through official
channels. It must have had the same effect that you'd get if a
total stranger approached you in the street and offered to issue
you with a passport. The natural reaction in first-century
Judaism to Jesus' declaration that someone's sins were forgiven
would be that he seemed to think he was the Temple-system –
building, priests, sacrifices, the lot – and especially that he
seemed to think he was in the position of the Shekinah itself.

This, actually, isn't a wildly odd idea in first-century Judaism.
The Essenes believed that their community was the true replace-
ment for the Jerusalem Temple. The Pharisees seem to have
thought that, in some senses at least, their ritual meals taken
together in strict purity enabled them to recapture, privately,
something of the sanctity you'd get by being in the Temple itself.
They suggested, too, that when people studied the Torah (Law)
it was as though they were in the very presence of the living God
himself. What Jesus was doing was not stepping outside Jewish

monotheism, with its normal variations, but acting within it in
such a way as to draw the eye up to himself. He was implicitly
taking the place of the Essene community, or of the Pharisees'
fellowship: *he* was the place where Israel was to meet her God.
This cannot be dismissed by saying it's a late idea, a Gentile
myth, a pagan invention, a Pauline muddle, or anything else.

Which 'One God' are we Talking About?

Of course, this way of looking at thing demands a different view
of 'God' from the one regularly held within the modern Western
world. That, I think, is where a good deal of the problem seems
to lie.

A couple of years ago I was part of a panel discussion in the
Sheldonian Theatre in Oxford. The interviewer tossed me the
question: 'Was Jesus God?' That's one of those trick questions
that you can't answer straight on. It assumes that we know what
'God' means, and we're simply asking if Jesus is somehow
identified with this 'God'. What we should say, instead, is: 'It all
depends what you mean by "God".' Well, what *do* people mean?

When people say 'God' today (apart from using the word as a
casual expletive) they are usually referring to a hypothetical
Being who lives at some distance from the world, detached from
normal life. This Being may occasionally intervene, but for the
most part stays aloof, watchful, vaguely disapproving.

Now if *that*'s the sort of view of 'God' you hold – and in my
experience it's pretty common – then of course to ask 'Is Jesus
God?' is laughable. Jesus was a full-blooded human being. As
Wilson is fond of pointing out, Jesus had a reputation for being a
party-goer, a drinker. The sort of company he kept made
reputable people – including his own family – look down their
noses with disapproval. It's ridiculous to think of Jesus as being
'God' in that high-and-dry sense, detached and disapproving. (If
you want to see what such a Jesus might look like, the B-grade
biblical movies of a few years ago will provide plenty of examples, with their dreary, dreamy Jesus-figures, who made lofty
pronouncements and stared into the middle distance as though
scanning the skies for angels.)

But supposing we started out with a different view of 'God'?
We could perfectly easily run through the options. What about a

Hindu God – a figure like Krishna, say? No, that doesn't look like Jesus either. What about a Muslim view of God, the stern Allah who demands total and blind obedience? No, that won't fit. But what about the Old Testament view of God?

In the Old Testament we find a God who yearns over the plight of his people, and indeed of the whole world. He hates the human wickedness which has defaced his world, and which destroys other humans, and its own perpetrators, as it goes along. Not to hate such wickedness would be, to say the least, morally culpable. But this Old Testament God is also one who, when people are in misery and at their wits' end, comes in person to deal with the problem. He rolls up his sleeves to get on with the job (Isaiah 52.10). (What Isaiah actually says is 'the LORD has bared his holy arm', but in my language that means that God rolled up his sleeves.) And Isaiah again, this time in chapter 63 verse 8, speaks of Israel's God sharing the distress and affliction of his people, and rescuing them personally.

Now: let us suppose that *this* God were to become human. What would such a God look like? Very much, I submit, like Jesus of Nazareth.[10] This is the really scary thing that writers like A. N. Wilson never come to grips with; not that Jesus might be identified with a remote, lofty, imaginary being (any fool could see the flaw in that idea), but that God, the real God, the one true God, might actually look like Jesus. And not a droopy, pre-Raphaelite Jesus, either, but a shrewd Palestinian Jewish villager who drank wine with his friends, agonized over the plight of his people, taught in strange stories and pungent aphorisms, and was executed by the occupying forces. What does that do to Christian belief?

The Christian doctrine of the incarnation was never intended to be about the elevation of a human being to divine status. That's what, according to some Romans, happened to the emperors after they died, or even before. The Christian doctrine is all about *a different sort of God* – a God who was so different to normal expectations that he could, completely appropriately, become human in, and as, the man Jesus of Nazareth. To say that Jesus is in some sense God is of course to make a startling statement about Jesus. It is also to make a stupendous claim about God.

Jesus and God

Once we grasp this possibility, there opens up before us a far better way of reading the early Christian language about God and Jesus than we find in Wilson's book. Wilson seems to be stuck in the belief (it's really a typical 1960s viewpoint) that the early church made Jesus divine by revising their Jewish beliefs in the light of pagan philosophical categories. It has to be said most emphatically that this simply isn't the case.

The evidence is actually quite clear. From the very earliest Christian documents we possess (i.e. the letters of Paul) right through mainstream Christianity to the fifth century and beyond, we find Christians straining every nerve to say what they found themselves compelled to say: *not* that there were now two, or three, different Gods, but that the one true God had revealed himself to be, within himself so to speak, irrevocably threefold. The whole point of the doctrine of the Trinity, both in its early stages in passages like Galatians 4.1–7, 1 Corinthians 12.4–6, 2 Corinthians 13.13, and Matthew 28.19, and in its later stages in the writings of the Greek and Latin Fathers, was that one could *not* say that there was a plurality of Gods: only that there was an irreducible threefold-ness about the one God. The Fathers drew on non-Christian philosophical categories, not to *invent* this belief, but to try to *explain* it to their contemporaries.

And, all the time, Christian belief in this one God was set over against the same paganism that Jewish monotheism had always opposed. What we find in early Christianity, in fact, is the same basic theological position that we find in Judaism: a belief in the one God of Abraham, Isaac and Jacob, who was to vindicate his name, and his people, against the pagan 'gods'. The difference is that, for the Jews, this vindication was still to come, when this God would give them a great political and military victory over their enemies. For the Christians, the vindication had already taken place, when God raised Jesus from the dead.

This, then, is Jewish monotheism as it actually was in the first century, and in its reuse in the early church. It was not, as Wilson constantly suggests, a technical, philosophers' analysis of the inner being of the one God, marking a decisive shift away from the beliefs of Jesus. It was a polemical belief in the one true God over against all false gods, all idols. Jesus shared this belief; so did all early Christians, not least Paul. But there was nothing

in it to stop them believing that the one true God was revealing
himself, and had revealed himself, in, and even *as*, Jesus.

What About the Future?

Jews of Jesus' day, it is constantly said, thought that the world
was about to come to a grinding halt. Quite what they thought
was going to happen next, received wisdom today is not so sure.
But, as we saw, a procession of scholars from Johannes Weiss
and Albert Schweitzer down to the present day has been quite
convinced that the Jews expected the end of the world. More:
they have been convinced that Jesus expected this too.

Jesus and the 'End'

If he did, then of course he was mistaken. The world has
rumbled on, lurching from crisis to crisis, but never actually
coming to an end, ever since. So, many have concluded, if Jesus
was wrong we must find a way of salvaging something from the
wreckage. This is the point at which many writers have turned
Jesus into either a moralist (the route Wilson takes) or an exist-
entialist (Bultmann's route). That is a way of having your cake
and eating it: of having Jesus, without the embarrassment of his
rather odd views about the immediate future.

One result, of course, of thinking that Jesus expected the
world to end is that he couldn't possibly have thought of anything so long-term as founding a church. At this point the
embarrassment of having a mistaken Jesus is overtaken by the
welcome prospect of having an anti-church Jesus. Wilson, who
combines the two, writes that if the idea of founding a church
had occurred to Jesus he would have regarded it as a Satanic
temptation (p. 111f.). But once again what we are faced with is a
total misreading of what first-century Judaism was actually like.

Jews and the 'End'

The funny thing about modern understandings of ancient
Judaism is that we have been taught to read highly coloured,

flowery flights of Jewish imagery as though they were plain, plodding prose. When we read a passage which says that 'the sun and the moon shall be darkened, and the stars shall not give their light', we ought to know, as my colleague Professor John Barton engagingly puts it, that the passage will not go on to say that 'the rest of the country will have sunny intervals and scattered showers'.[11] The language simply doesn't work like that.

Read the Old Testament, and you will see how this sort of imagery is used. It is a way of talking about what *we* would call 'earth-shattering events'. Of course, when we use a phrase like that, we don't mean that the earth has been literally shattered. The devaluation of sterling in September 1992 was a fairly earth-shattering event for British financiers, and especially for the Government. But if anyone, reading that last sentence, were to imagine that a huge earthquake had struck London, destroying the financial district, and causing serious cracks to appear in the Parliament building, we would smile and point out that the language is *metaphorical*. 'Earth-shattering events' are, in fact, sometimes more important, historically and politically speaking, than mere earthquakes.

When Jewish writers spoke of the sun and moon being darkened; when they spoke of angels gathering people from the four winds of heaven; when, in particular, they spoke of a Son of Man who would come on the clouds of heaven – in each of these cases they were using language in this metaphorical way. It is flagrantly absurd to think that Jesus, in saying that sort of thing, envisaged himself or anyone else literally flying around in mid-air on an actual cloud. This is well-known first-century imagery, and what it means is something like this: (a) the people of God are being oppressed by pagan foes; (b) God will vindicate them soon; (c) when this happens the effect will be (in our language) 'earth-shattering', resulting in God's people being set in a position of authority over the rest of humankind.

This means that a lot of Wilson's rhetoric, about the absurdity of believing in Jesus flying around on a cloud, simply misses the point, as do similar discussions in some more scholarly literature. This 'Son of Man' language does not mean that Jesus is being regarded as a 'supernatural figure', such as no serious first-century Jew could believe in. The language in question refers to this-worldly events, to things that happen in ordinary space and time, particularly in the rough-and-tumble of social, cultural, political and military affairs. The purpose of the highly charged metaphors about 'beasts', 'clouds', and 'Son of Man' is to *invest* events of that sort with their real theological *significance*.

It is quite clear from our old friend Josephus that many Jews of Jesus' day did think like this, not least in terms of a worldwide Jewish kingdom that would be the end-product of the great event that was coming. They didn't expect the end of the world; merely the end of *the present way the world was run*. Soon the pagans would be put in their place, and the Jews (or at least the faithful, Torah-observing Jews) would be put in authority. There are, indeed, some signs that Wilson has recognized this point, as we shall see presently.

Hope for the Kingdom

All this is in direct line with the Old Testament. Abraham had been promised that in his family all the families of the earth would be blessed (Genesis 12.3). The Psalms sing of Israel's coming King as having a dominion stretching from one end of the world to the other (Psalm 72.8). The book of Isaiah speaks of Israel and/or her King as the light of the world (Isaiah 11.1–10; 42.1–6; 60.1–22). Right through Israel's history there had been a sense that, strange though it might seem, the one true God would use this small and apparently insignificant nation as his means of transforming the entire world.

This great transforming event would be, finally, *the coming of the Kingdom of God*. Here again Wilson's account, like (it has to be said) many modern scholarly treatments of the question, is not sufficiently grounded in first-century Judaism. It is clear, again from Josephus and elsewhere, that the idea of God's becoming King was not about an inner set of ideals, a 'Kingdom' invisible to the naked eye but quietly transforming people's inner motivations. It was about the expected dramatic reversal in Israel's fortunes. To say, as many Jewish revolutionaries did, that there should be 'no King but God', was a way of saying that Caesar, Herod and Pontius Pilate should not be ruling the people of this God. God himself would rule, presumably through his appointed delegates, certainly through a properly constituted priesthood in the Jerusalem Temple – and, quite probably, through a true King, a Messiah.

Jesus transformed the notion of God's Kingdom, to be sure. But he never made it purely an inward, private thing, a matter of a shift in motivation or a new inner attitude. It was still emphatically to do with the way in which Israel's God was to become Lord of all the world. What Wilson never sees is that it was not out of line, not particularly unexpected, that a first-century Jew should get it into his head that the one true God was going to establish his Kingdom *here*, *now*, and was going to do so precisely through the work of this same first-century Jew. On the contrary: we know of several messianic movements in the hundred years before and after Jesus, and there is every reason to think that several of the would-be Messiahs did think pretty much like this.

Messiahship

There was, after all, nothing particularly surprising in ordinary human beings thinking that they might be the Messiah. That of itself certainly didn't mean that the person in question was thinking of himself as *divine*. One of the most persistent mistakes throughout the literature on Jesus in the last hundred years is to use the word 'Christ', which simply means 'Messiah', as though it was a 'divine' title (as in 'The Jesus of History and the Christ of Faith', or 'Jesus Who Became Christ'). If Jesus thought of himself as Messiah, this is a completely different matter to the possibility, which we explored a moment ago, that he might have believed that Israel's God was active in and through him in a unique way. If we can get this separation clear, we will have done the debate a great service.

The transformation Jesus effected within the expectation of the Kingdom, and the hope for a coming Messiah, did not involve giving them up altogether. Rather, it meant radically redrawing them, focusing them on Jesus' own suffering and death. Wilson here comes a hedge's breadth away from grasping the point, only to look in the wrong direction at the critical moment. This, I think, is the most poignant fact about his whole book.

Jesus, then, did not think the world would come to an end. If
he had, his fellow Jews wouldn't have known what on earth to
make of such a crank, since what they were longing for was for
their God to act *within* continuing history, and bring them out on
top. Jesus did, however, think that Israel's God was going to
establish his Kingdom *through his* (that is, Jesus') *own work*. How
this worked out in practice remains to be seen.

Wilson's Portrait of Jesus

After the fireworks and the flourish of trumpets of Wilson's
opening chapters, his portrait of Jesus is, frankly, something of a
disappointment. He sees a good deal, but never puts it together
into a clear, coherent, historically credible, or even very attractive, package.

His Jesus is a moralist: 'Be Better Jews' is one summary of
the 'prophetic' message which he, like his predecessors, had
preached (p. 106f.). 'Make the men sit down,' he said to the disciples prior to feeding the 5,000 in the wilderness. Wilson makes
a great deal of this: here is a crowd ready to rise in revolt, ready
to march on Jerusalem, and Jesus symbolically gets them to sit
down. (This also enables Wilson to make great play, on p. 161,
of the contrast between the men sitting down and 'Damsel,
arise', which Jesus said to Jairus' daughter – as though Jesus had
a worked-out policy of 'suppressing the yang and exalting the
yin'.) This is a way of doing what many writers have done:
highlighting one interesting feature and making it do duty for a
good deal that is missed out. This is the sign of caricature, not of
real history.

As we saw, Wilson's Jesus 'dreamed of a simple Judaism,
stripped of its besetting sins of moralism and sectarianism'
(p. 187). 'He preaches the union of Israel, its mystic and
indissoluble communion, and he urges the sectarians to put their
differences aside' (p. 163). That is an interesting sentence. It
comes, by way of literary allusion, from a Christian hymn:

> Yet she on earth hath union
> With God the Three in One,
> And mystic sweet communion
> With those whose rest is won . . .[12]

What is Wilson, of all people, doing summarizing the message of this explicitly trinitarian and church-supporting hymn, and attributing it to the Jesus of history?

Even when we strip away these later allusions and penetrate to the generalized moralism beneath, the ideas Wilson attributes to Jesus sound, frankly, more like the message of Johanan ben Zakkai, who refounded Rabbinic Judaism after the fall of Jerusalem in AD 70, than like Jesus of Nazareth. They also run the risk of restating a view of Judaism which E. P. Sanders has more or less demolished. First-century Judaism, we now see clearly, was not 'moralistic' in the sense that we today understand 'moralism', i.e. earning one's ticket to salvation by being good. Certainly it took the divine law very seriously. But it had little in common with the kind of self-help 'moralism' which has earned the word a bad name in recent centuries. What we are left with, from Wilson's portrait, is a Jesus who is a mildly interesting figure, as historical personages go, but who is scarcely worth worrying about, then or now.

Resurrection

Wilson may well want to reply that this is just the point. Jesus is interesting, but not worth the sort of fuss the church has made of him. To this suggestion the crucial reply must focus on the resurrection.

What Happened at Easter?

It has always been central to the church's faith that the true God raised Jesus from the dead. Something, it is agreed on all sides, happened shortly after Jesus' death which transformed the situation from one of apparent defeat to one in which a new movement came to birth. As historians of whatever background, we are bound (as we saw in the first chapter) to ask: granted the life and death of Jesus, why did the early church get going, and why did it take the shape it did? There is a hole in the historical jigsaw-puzzle at just this point. One major test of any hypothesis about the history of the first century is how well it can cope with this hole. What does Wilson do?

Red Herrings and Blind Alleys

First, he manages to spread a certain amount of confusion by dragging the late Professor Morton Smith into the argument. Smith claimed to have discovered a tiny fragment of text which, he argued, was part of an early version of Mark's gospel. In this text, a scantily-clad young man comes to Jesus by night for a strange magical initiation. Perhaps, Smith suggested, this is a clue to the real nature of Jesus and his first followers, before the later church hushed it all up.

Wilson admits, as most scholars of all backgrounds will readily agree, that this strange scrap of writing is extremely unlikely to belong to anything more than a very late fantasy-work. But it allows him to suggest that maybe there were, in the early church, rituals of some sort involving ceremonial 'dying' and 'rising'. Maybe that is what lies behind the story of the raising of Lazarus in John 11. And if so, maybe . . . that is what lies behind the story of the resurrection of Jesus, too. After all, Wilson says, there are several other 'raisings' in the gospels. Not only Lazarus and Jairus' daughter, and the widow's son at Nain; John the Baptist is thought by Herod to have been raised to life, too, precisely in the person of Jesus himself (on this, see p. 103). What more natural, then, than that Jesus' followers should eventually come to believe that he was raised to life?

What more *un*natural, frankly. Those who believed that Jairus' daughter was raised to life believed it because she was alive, there with them. Those who believed in the raising of Lazarus did so because he was alive again. In neither case, interestingly, did anyone draw from the event the conclusions that were drawn from Jesus' resurrection. Nobody said that Lazarus was therefore the Son of God, or Jairus' daughter, therefore the Daughter of God. That alone serves to distinguish (as Wilson does not) these two events, on the one hand, from Jesus' resurrection, on the other. The only sense we can make of what the early Christians were saying about Jesus is that they thought, not that he had simply returned from the dead into ordinary human life, but that he had passed through death into a new territory somewhere beyond. There was nothing commonplace or ordinary about that sort of affirmation.

Another Strange Hypothesis

The crucial question about Lazarus, and Jairus' daughter, as Wilson sees in the case of the girl, was: were they really dead? According to the gospels, yes; according to Wilson, no. In the case of Jesus, however, Wilson has no doubt that Jesus really did die on the cross. What then happened, he says, was that Jesus' brother James, who hadn't been particularly involved with the disciples up to that point, showed up and spoke to them. Somehow they got confused and thought he was Jesus, alive again. This 'explains' the confusion among the disciples as to who the stranger was on the road to Emmaus, or in the garden. ('If . . . the stranger were not the dear friend, but the dear friend's brother, who bore a strong resemblance, then this is just the sort of "double take" which we should expect' (p. 244).)

This is, frankly, such a tissue of nonsense that it is hard to know where to begin to answer it. For a start, the place of James in the early church was quite different from the place accorded to the risen Lord. By all accounts, James was a key player in the early years of church history, and people would soon have discovered if the one they thought was the risen Lord turned out to be his brother.[13] In the very earliest writing about the resurrection (1 Corinthians 15), James himself is listed as one of the people to whom the risen Lord appeared. But the real issue lies deeper, with the notion of 'resurrection' itself.

Bodily Resurrection: Jewish Belief

It cannot be stressed too strongly that 'resurrection', for Jews of the period, had nothing to do with mere resuscitation. It was not a matter of coming back into the same sort of life. It was a matter of going through death, and out into a new world beyond. In the nature of the case, we don't have much information about this new world. But one thing we do know. The whole mainline Judaeo-Christian tradition insists that in this new world people will have *bodies*. Whatever else will be true of them, they will still be *physical*.

These bodies may not be exactly the same as the present ones. Paul, in trying to explain this, uses the dramatic image of a seed and a plant (1 Corinthians 15.35–8). The present body has to die; the new one will emerge from it. 'Resurrection', then, is not the same as 'resuscitation'. Nor is it the same as the immortality, or the transmigration, of a disembodied soul or spirit. It is what the Maccabean martyrs of the second century BC were longing for when they spoke of Israel's God giving them back their limbs and organs after they had suffered horrible torture and death. People who believe that sort of thing would not be prepared to use the word 'resurrection' unless something emphatically physical had taken place.

Equally, it must be stressed that first-century Jews were not expecting people to rise from the dead (in this sense) simply as isolated individuals, on a one-off basis, here and there. Herod's remark about Jesus being a resurrected John the Baptist does not represent mainline Jewish belief. 'Resurrection', for them, was something that would happen to all dead Jews, and perhaps all dead humans. It would happen on the great future occasion when the True God (who after all was the creator of the world) finally brought history round its last great corner, into the new day that was about to dawn. 'Resurrection', in other words, was about God's restoration of his whole people, about his coming Kingdom, about the great reversal of fortune for Israel and the world. It was about the birth of a whole new world order.

The Vital Question

The vital question that must then be addressed is: *why then did the earliest Christians use this word about Jesus*? What was it that caused Jews who believed all this to claim that Jesus had experienced 'resurrection', as a single individual within history?

It is clear that nothing had occurred which would make them think that Israel had suddenly become the ruler of the world. No event had happened on the social, political or military stage to make them think that at last the long night of pagan oppression had come to an end. If we bracket off the resurrection itself, the only other recent event of significance had been the execution of yet another apparent messianic pretender. That was a common enough phenomenon. It communicated to the Jews, not that the Kingdom had come, but that it clearly had not.

It will not do to say, as many have done, that the disciples had a wonderful inner experience and sense of the love and grace and forgiveness of God. This was the argument used by the Dutch theologian Edward Schillebeeckx in his huge book on Jesus.[14] Jews quite often experienced God's love and grace in new, fresh and illuminating ways, not least after passing through times of crisis and pain. They had several well-developed ways of talking about this sort of experience. There is no evidence whatsoever that they would use 'resurrection' language in such a situation. Especially, there is no evidence that, faced with the catastrophic destruction of their hopes in the death of a would-be leader or Messiah, Jews who found their hearts once more strangely warmed by a sense of the love of Israel's God would say, of this person, that he had been raised from the dead.

It will not do, therefore, to say that Jesus' disciples were so stunned and shocked by his death, so unable to come to terms with it, that they projected their shattered hopes onto the screen of fantasy and invented the idea of Jesus' 'resurrection' as a way of coping with a cruelly broken dream. That has an initial apparent psychological plausibility, but it won't work as serious first-century history. We know of lots of other messianic and similar movements in the Jewish world roughly contemporary with Jesus. In many cases the leader died a violent death at the hands of the authorities. In not one single case do we hear the slightest mention of the disappointed followers claiming that their hero had been raised from the dead. They knew better. 'Resurrection' was not a private event. It involved human bodies. There would have to be an empty tomb somewhere. A Jewish revolutionary whose leader had been executed by the authorities, and who managed to escape arrest himself, had two options: give up the revolution, or find another leader. We have evidence of people doing both. Claiming that the original leader was alive again was simply not an option.

Unless, of course, he was.

A. N. Wilson: Weighing the Evidence

Wilson's Jesus is a pale and distorted version of the real thing. The portrait is something of a caricature: some of the features are there all right, and some indeed are finely drawn. But so many are missing, and so many are out of shape, that it is only just recognizable. And I do not mean 'recognizable within orthodox Christianity'. I mean 'recognizable as serious history'.

According to the standards Wilson himself sets up, therefore, his book has to be judged a failure. It has some moving moments, and poses some of the right questions. But as a whole, and in a good many of its parts, it simply does not convince. It reads as what it manifestly is, in the light of Wilson's other writings and his much-publicized abandoning of Christianity. It is his attempt to think through the implications of a position he has reached on quite different grounds.

There is, of course, nothing wrong with that. It is what scientists do when conducting an experiment to test a hypothesis. It is what historians do all the time, testing a theory by a fresh examination of the evidence. Many of us, indeed, sense a continuing obligation to work through the implications of a position which we find ourselves wanting to embrace. But the proof of the pudding is in the eating. Does this working through actually end up making sense, producing a coherent whole? Or does it leave us feeling that there are more loose ends than we started with? I have no doubt that in the case of this book the second of these is true. I hope that Wilson himself will come to recognize this, and will think again about Jesus. If he has changed his mind once, there is no reason why he should not do so again.

4

John Spong: The Bishop and the Birth

Shepherds and Mangers: Cards, Carols and Controversy

John Selby Spong is Bishop of Newark in New Jersey. He has made his name by championing causes that have left traditionalists in the church reeling. Whether it is the ordination of practising homosexuals, or the denial of the literal, bodily resurrection of Jesus; whether it is radically redefining what morality really is, or (in his own phrase) 'rescuing the Bible from fundamentalism', John Spong is ready with articulate, well-constructed and plausible arguments. *The Guardian* said of one of his books: 'It is the most lucid and erudite statement of non-literal faith since Bishop John Robinson's *Honest to God*.' An Australian periodical simply said: 'Thank God for Spong.'

Not everyone will agree with this last sentiment, especially when they read his new book, *Born of a Woman: A Bishop Rethinks the Birth of Jesus*.[1] In it he presents five arguments in particular. (a) The biblical stories of Jesus' birth are 'midrash', that is, fanciful stories which weren't meant to be taken literally. (b) The idea of the literal truth of the Bible has contributed to the long-standing male dominance in the church, which has forced women to fit a stereotyped set of roles and expectations, not least that of motherhood. (c) The virgin birth, in particular, was not literally true, since Mary was quite likely the victim of rape. (d) *Belief in* the virgin birth has contributed to an artificial and destructive view of women. (e) Jesus was quite probably married, most likely to Mary Magdalene.

Spong presents this case with his usual lucidity, and with a constant pietistic refrain. In several of his chapters, he swings round at the end, away from the negative statements of all that we cannot or must not believe, to a sermonic mode in which he

makes devotional capital out of the beliefs that he offers as
replacements for the traditional ones.

Spong knows his way round a certain amount of biblical
scholarship. He has clearly spent time over many years studying
both primary and secondary sources, and interacting with many
biblical scholars on both sides of the Atlantic. Unlike A. N. Wilson, therefore, one senses that he has done a lot more than
simply draw on a few recent writings that suit his point of view.
In particular, he leans heavily at point after point on the work of
the American Roman Catholic scholar Raymond Brown, whose
major book *The Birth of the Messiah*[2] is the standard work on the
infancy narratives in Matthew and Luke. (Brown, of course, ends
up with a position very different to that of Spong himself; Spong
explains this by saying, somewhat patronizingly, that Brown is of
course so deeply enmeshed in his own tradition that he cannot
break out of it.) Spong is, to this extent, in a different league
from Wilson. Unlike Thiering's work, his book does indeed
reflect more or less what a good many people in some parts of
the church think, even if it is expressed more starkly than many
others would dare to do.

There are, nevertheless, several points at which his account
must be challenged. We may begin with the two which are the
foundations of everything else he does.

Literal and Theological Truth

When Spong wages a running battle with 'those who take the
Bible literally', it soon becomes clear what his real target is.
There are, he writes, lots of 'simple believers', 'to whom the
television evangelists direct their appeal'. The latter, he says,

> offer to their legions biblical security, certainty in faith, and
> even superiority in their sense of salvation. In return, their
> supporters provide the evangelists with a following that can
> be translated into political power and enormous financial
> resources ... That electronic power assures that religious
> ignorance will continue to live for yet a while longer (p. 3f.).

Spong admits that he himself grew up as a biblical fundamentalist, with the Bible becoming a part of his very being. When he

abandoned fundamentalism, though, he did not cease to love the Bible and study it intensely. This has led him into a variety of non-literal ways of reading the Bible, since on its apparent surface meaning it produces all sorts of contradictions. (In setting out some of these contradictions, Spong is sometimes guilty of gross caricature: for instance, whoever thought that Lot's behaviour in offering his daughters to the mob in Sodom was part of 'biblical morality'? Certainly not the author/redactor of Genesis 19.[3]) Constantly throughout the book he reiterates the difference between a 'merely literal' reading of the text and a deeper, apparently richer, more 'theological' reading. Thus he writes on pp. 11–13:

A literalized myth is a doomed myth. Its truth cannot be rescued. Literalism is not even a benign alternative for contemporary Christians. It is, in the modern world, nothing less than an enemy to faith in Jesus Christ . . . Literalism is a claim that God's eternal truth has been, or can be, captured in the time-limited concepts of human history . . . The day has passed for me when, in the name of tolerance to the religious insecurities of others, I will allow my Christ to be defined inside a killing literalism . . . The time has come for the church to surrender its neurotic pattern of trafficking in one feeble religious security system after another and to allow its people to feel the bracing wind of insecurity, so that Christians might understand what it means to walk by faith.

It is at points like this that one begins to feel what the *Guardian* might have meant in likening Spong to the John Robinson of *Honest to God*. That book contained the same passion, the same odd mixture of rhetoric and eclectic theology, and the same standing of ordinary Christian language on its head. Like A. N. Wilson, Spong sometimes sounds like a 1960s' man born (or at least writing) out of due time. In particular, talk of 'my Christ' is the kind of thing that, as Spong must realize, leaves him wide open to the charge of sheer subjectivism – especially when it is combined with a continual downplaying of historical truth. How do we know that Spong's 'Christ' is the real Christ?

The most important thing to be said here, however, is that I, and the great majority of Christians known to me, will very readily agree with Spong in his rejection both of a fundamentalism that insists on 'taking everything literally' and of a liberalism that takes nothing in the Bible with any seriousness at all. This, however, leaves us with a wide range of positions from which to choose. I agree with Spong precisely in wanting to take the Bible very seriously but in a thoroughly non-fundamentalist way; but what does this mean in practice?

Avoiding Fundamentalism

The fundamentalism to which Spong objects does indeed exist throughout the contemporary world, almost as a balancing polar opposite of the new phenomenon known as 'post-modernism'.[4] It is not, however, nearly so widespread in England (for instance) as it is in America. In my experience, many of the people who fulminate against 'fundamentalists' have little or no first-hand experience of the phenomenon they so hate – except sometimes, as Spong admits is true of himself, in their own earlier years. The word 'fundamentalism' has thus become a way of dismissing anyone who places more weight on the Bible than one does oneself. As such, it is fairly useless.

Let us be clear about some basics. There *is* such a thing as a spurious emphasis on 'literal truth' in passages where the Bible demonstrably intends poetry, metaphor and so on. This emphasis must be identified, using proper critical methods, and carefully left to one side.

There *is* such a thing as a longing for security in our wildly insecure modern world, and a transfer of that longing to the 'religious' sphere, with the result that religious arguments are provided as a rationalization of the political or social status quo. Such arguments (which are not confined, incidentally, to those known as 'fundamentalists') must be identified and exposed for what they are.

There *is* such a thing as a worldview which oppresses all who do not conform to it, and which, as part of this, insists on stereotyped roles for men and women. Any attempt to use the Bible to back up such dehumanizing stereotypes must be firmly resisted – though, again, there is more than one way of dehumanizing people by insisting on stereotyped roles.

There is, in other words, such a phenomenon as fundamentalism. I suspect that Spong has seen – from the inside as well as the outside – a good deal more of it than I have. But this does not justify him in constantly labelling in this way any attempt to understand the Bible as referring to things that actually happened within history. As we saw earlier, this division between history and faith is basically unhelpful. It emerges throughout Spong's discussion, imposing a flat 'either–or' on the material where a more sensitive reader would be bound to say 'both-and'. Thus, for example, Spong insists that Jesus must be *either* divine *or* human, characterizing the Jesus of church tradition as 'the nonhuman Jesus of later Christian mythology', and adding that this figure 'is found in the birth narratives of Matthew and Luke' (p. 21). We need to trace further where all this has come from.

History and Faith

We saw earlier that the split between history and faith goes back at least as far as the eighteenth century, when Lessing wrote of the 'ugly ditch' between historical truth and eternal truth. There is a good deal of Lessing in Spong – just at the time, ironically, when the worldview which Lessing represents is emphatically on the way out in the Western world. The church, as so often, climbs on the bandwagon just when the wheels are coming off.

But Spong's repeated either–or, of literal readings of the Bible versus non-literal, goes back a lot further than that in the history of the church. Here the irony is even deeper. Spong constantly wages war against the Fathers of the church in the early centuries of Christianity, who (he says) got the early message of Jesus and Paul muddled up by imposing pagan categories on to them. What he does not seem to realize is that his own distinction, between the literal truth of the Bible and some other, non-literal, meanings, is precisely the analytical tool employed by some of those same Fathers to bring about their particular understanding. The very Fathers who promoted non-literal readings of the Bible most assiduously are the same ones who also promoted a 'high' view of Jesus, so high as to run the apparent risk of making him less than human.

Spong's non-literal reading of the Bible, therefore, puts him on all fours with the great allegorizers like Clement of Alexandria (*c*.150–215), who argued (among other things) that Jesus, being divine, did not need to eat or drink, but merely did so to keep up appearances and avoid worrying the disciples. Clement, one of the Fathers who most obviously imported Greek ideas into the early church, is presumably one of those whom Spong attacks when he says that the idea of incarnation 'arises out of a Greek dualism' (p. 25). Does Spong realize, I wonder, that in embracing non-literal meanings of Scripture he is following exactly those very theologians whose findings he professes elsewhere to abominate?

The irony goes deeper still. One of the great emphases of the sixteenth-century Protestant Reformation was the primacy of the literal sense of the Bible, over against the free-for-all allegorical readings that had developed in some parts of the church in the Middle Ages. One would have thought that Spong would have rejected this Reformation emphasis, and exalted the earlier medieval multi-layered readings which correspond so much more closely, at the level of method, to what he is advocating. He seems, however, to approve heartily of the Reformation. Why? Because, according to him, pre-Reformation Christianity produced a denigration of women that is still visible in some quarters, whereas the Reformation produced 'a rebellion against that traditional definition of women', setting them free to break the mould and emerge as people in their own right.

This case, which I would have thought was fairly dubious historically, is made rhetorically even more so by his chosen example of the latter phenomenon: Margaret Thatcher (p. 220f.). That aside, his method still seems to me to be full of holes. Anything that the sixteenth-century Reformers achieved, they did precisely by insisting on the literal sense of Scripture over against wild allegorizing. Where does that leave Spong?

Spong's blanket denunciation of the literal reading of Scripture leaves him wide open to the charge that, without a literal sense as the anchor, the Bible can be made to mean anything at all. When, in his concluding chapters, we find the confident suggestions that Mary was pregnant with Jesus because she had been raped, and that Jesus was married to Mary Magdalene, it becomes clear that this is precisely what is happening. As so often with theology born of reaction, Spong's violent dislike for the fundamentalism which he used to embrace has led him into gross overstatement.

What, then, of his great claim, that the birth narratives belong to the genre 'midrash'?

The Gospels and 'Midrash'

What is 'Midrash'?

Throughout his book, Spong uses the category of 'midrash'. I shall let him explain it in his own words (pp. 18–20):

> The way the Jewish tradition viewed and treated Scripture was very clear. This method produced what was called midrash. Midrash represented efforts on the part of the rabbis to probe, tease, and dissect the sacred story looking for hidden meanings, filling in blanks, and seeking clues to yet-to-be-revealed truth . . .
> The readers of the Gospels who understood this midrashic method of probing Scripture would understand. Only to a generation living hundreds of years later, separated from their Jewish religious roots and clinging to a peculiarly Western mind-set, would the choice appear to be between literal truth and overt lies . . .
> The Gospels, far more than we have thought before, are examples of Christian midrash. In the Gospels, the ancient Jewish story would be shaped, retold, interpreted, and even changed so as to throw proper light on the person of Jesus. There was nothing objective about the Gospel tradition. These were not biographies. They were books designed to inspire faith.
> To force these narratives into the straitjacket of literal historicity is to violate their intention, their method, and their truth. To see them as expressions of the genre called midrash with a Christian twist is to enter Scripture in a new and perhaps a life-giving way.

There are some fairly obvious oddities on the surface of this account. If there is anything clear about first-century Jewish exegesis of Scripture, it is that nothing is clear about it. If the first generation to misread the midrashic gospels was really 'hundreds of years later', a good deal of Spong's polemic against the second-generation church, not least Matthew and Luke, loses its point. But these issues are not central.

What is central is that Spong apparently does not know what 'midrash' actually is. The 'genre' of writing to which he makes such confident appeal is nothing at all like he says it is. There is such a thing as 'midrash'; scholars have been studying it, discussing it, and analysing it, for years. Spong seems to be unaware of the most basic results of this study. He has grabbed the word out of the air, much as Barbara Thiering grabbed the idea of 'pesher' exegesis, and to much the same effect. He misunderstands the method itself, and uses this bent tool to make the gospels mean what he wants instead of what they say.

Let me be clear. I am *not* saying that the gospels, and the birth narratives, have only a flat, literal meaning. That would be absurd. I have made it clear in various writings that they are written with great artistry at the level of narrative and theology.[5] There are depths to them which the crude literalist is bound to miss, to his or her great loss. But *they are not midrash.*

This has become clear from the work of the great contemporary writers in the field. Names like Geza Vermes and Jacob Neusner come to mind: Spong doesn't mention them in his discussion of midrash, perhaps not surprisingly, since although they are the acknowledged experts on the subject, their work leaves no room for his strange distorted view.[6] The recently translated work of Strack and Stemberger, a classic treatment of the subject, finds no place in Spong either; nor do the very important studies of Philip Alexander, the Director of the Hebrew Studies Centre at Yarnton, Oxford.[7] Alexander's articles form, in fact, a direct and devastating rebuttal of the use of 'midrash' by Michael Goulder and others, upon whom Spong places great reliance.

Midrash and the Gospels

We may briefly indicate the ways in which genuine 'midrash' differs drastically from anything that we find in the gospels.

First, midrash proper consists of a commentary on an actual biblical text. It is not simply a fanciful retelling, but a careful discussion in which the original text itself remains clearly in focus. It is obvious that the gospels do not read in any way like this.

Second, real midrash is 'tightly controlled and argued'.[8] This is in direct opposition to Spong's idea of it, according to which (p. 184) 'once you enter the midrash tradition, the imagination is freed to roam and to speculate'. This statement tells us a good deal about Spong's own method of doing history, and nothing whatever about midrash. The use made of the Old Testament in the early chapters of Luke, to take an example, is certainly not midrash; neither is it roaming or speculative imagination.

Third, real midrash is a commentary precisely on Scripture. Goulder's theories, on which Spong professes to rely quite closely, suggest that Luke and Matthew were providing midrash on Mark. It is, however, fantastically unlikely that either of them would apply to Mark a technique developed for commenting on ancient Scripture.[9]

Fourth, midrash never included the invention of stories which were clearly seen as non-literal in intent, and merely designed to evoke awe and wonder. It was no part of Jewish midrash, or any other Jewish writing-genre in the first century, to invent all kinds of new episodes about recent history in order to advance the claim that the Scriptures had been fulfilled. It is one of the salient characteristics of Jewish literature throughout the New Testament period that, even though novelistic elements could creep in to books like Jubilees, the basic emphasis remains on that which happened *within history*.[10]

Where does this leave Spong's continued emphasis on 'midrash' as the correct literary genre for the gospels? In tatters. As Alexander says, in demolishing some of those on whom Spong relies:

> labelling a piece of Bible exegesis 'midrash' appears to set it in a definite historical and cultural context, to hint at well-known, technical parallels. But all this may be entirely bogus.[11]

There is, obviously, the possibility of genuine positive identification. Some of the Letter to the Hebrews could quite properly be considered in this light. But in the case of Spong there can be no doubt. He has followed a blind alley to a dead end. The gospels are not midrash.

The Gospels as Biography

In fact, despite his assertion to the contrary, the gospels are biographies. This comes as a shock to those who studied the

Bible in the 1950s and 1960s, when it was still a scholars' dogma, to be accepted uncritically on pain of exclusion from the guild, that the gospels were *not* biographies. This dogma grew up, as rigid as anything in older pre-critical systems, as part of precisely that distinction between faith and history which Spong, like A. N. Wilson, has uncritically embraced. It was not so much that scholars had examined ancient biographies and concluded that the gospels were not that sort of thing at all. It was more that the gospels were believed to be faith-documents; *therefore they could not be about history.*

Serious historical research, however, now indicates strongly that the gospels do indeed belong to the genre 'biography'. Of course, they are not just that. They contain a good deal besides. But they are *not less than* biographies. The most recent book on the subject has examined a good many biographies from the Greco-Roman world of the New Testament period, and has come up with this as its firm and positive conclusion.[12]

There is now, therefore, no reason to say that the writers of the gospels, and their very first readers, did not expect them to be taken as accounts of things that actually happened within history. To study their many other levels – symbolic, theological, sociological, literary – remains a fascinating and fruitful task. But as we engage with these levels we must not forget that the gospels would have appeared to a first-century reader, whether Jewish or non-Jewish, as books which told the story of an actual person who had lived and died in recent memory. We cannot escape from the problems that this creates by saying that they are of a different genre.

Jesus and Paul

One of the most fascinating contrasts between the books of Wilson and Spong is that they give us totally different accounts of Paul and his role in developing Christianity. For Wilson, Paul is the great villain who introduced wicked pagan ideas into the pure, early, Jewish message of Jesus himself, and who then passed them on to the gospel writers. For Spong, Paul is the great early writer who maintained the Jewish emphasis of the original message, and whose insights were completely lost by the evangelists! Faced with this, the average reader may want to give up in despair. How can we get at the truth if two writers tell us such diametrically opposite things?

The answer, of course, is that both are right and both are wrong. There isn't room here to argue this case out fully, but that isn't actually necessary. The texts will speak for themselves, once we have cleared away the basic misconceptions.

Wilson is absolutely right to see that Paul has a 'high' view of Jesus. As we saw, Paul includes the human being Jesus of Nazareth (not some non-human 'divine being') within his definition of the one true God. Here Spong cannot be allowed to slide around the relevant texts, as he does in the third chapter of his book, repeating the argument (which we earlier saw to be spurious) that no good Jewish monotheist could put Jesus into the same category as God.

Spong is absolutely right, however, to see that Paul refused to give ground to paganism. He remained a thoroughly Jewish thinker. At this point Wilson cannot be allowed to maintain that just because Paul believed in the incarnation, therefore he must have been a pagan at heart.

What matters is to recognize, as neither writer does, that in the very early period of the church's life there arose a firm, vital and healthy belief that Jesus was the true and final revelation of the one true God of Jewish monotheism. He was that to which the Jewish ideas of the Temple, the Word, the divine Wisdom, and so on, all pointed. You couldn't understand this doctrine in pagan terms without falsifying it at once. It was a totally Jewish doctrine – and yet it burst the boundaries of first-century Judaism.

In particular, Spong has moved right off limits when he says (p. 26) that Paul 'stood as a witness to a normal human birth process for Jesus'. This is a remarkable statement. Spong knows, as every careful reader of Paul knows, that there is simply no discussion of Jesus' birth in Paul. He has allowed himself to argue implicitly as follows:

Paul is a very Jewish thinker;
Jewish thinkers wouldn't assert that Jesus was conceived without a human father;
Therefore Paul thought Jesus' birth was normal in every way.

Unfortunately for Spong, this logic goes way beyond the evidence. The fact that in the two passages in which Paul mentions Jesus' birth (Galatians 4.4; Romans 1.3) he says nothing about the mode of conception proves nothing either way.

It is perfectly true that Paul's belief in Jesus' divinity did not depend on his embracing a particular view of how he was conceived or born. It was clearly possible to hold an incarnational theology as strong as Paul's without buttressing it with such ideas. But this should simply give us pause before we jump too readily to the conclusion that stories about the virginal conception are intended as part of a theology of incarnation. It is to this whole topic, the main focus of Spong's book, that we must now turn.

Born of a Virgin?

The resurrection is one great focus of current debate about Jesus. Wilson, as we have seen, discusses it in some detail. So does Spong, with similar results, which he has spelled out in an earlier book (*The Easter Moment*). There is no space here to go again into this debate, which we made a central point of the preceding chapter.

The other great focus of attention, predictably but perhaps regrettably, is the so-called virgin birth. I once heard Professor Ed Sanders, in an academic paper, refer to the current flurry of interest 'in Mary's hymen and Jesus' corpse'. There might, perhaps, have been less indelicate ways of putting it, but he was right enough to highlight these issues as the eye-catching ones. We must now turn our attention to this second issue.[13]

Conception and Birth

First things first. Technical terms are sometimes a nuisance, but sometimes they're vital. This is one of the latter cases.

The 'virgin birth' is better described as the virginal *conception*. It's one thing to ask how Jesus was *conceived*: Matthew and Luke say that this took place without a human father, i.e. while Mary remained a virgin. It's quite another to say, as the Bible does not but some Christians have, that Mary retained her virginity through the birth-process. That is not our present concern.

Nor should the virginal conception of Jesus be confused with the Roman Catholic doctrine of the 'immaculate conception' of Mary herself. That doctrine states that, when Mary herself was conceived, she was entirely free of original sin. That is completely non-biblical, and reflects much later belief-systems which have nothing intrinsically to do with Jesus himself.

This brings into focus one of several other preliminary points that must be made. To affirm that when Jesus was conceived no human father was involved, as traditional Christianity has always done, is *not* to make any statement or value-judgment whatsoever about sexuality – or sexual relations between married persons – being intrinsically evil. That is a dualist idea which some parts of the church have at some times embraced, but it is no part of true Christian teaching. I suspect that the natural interest in matters to do with sex is what keeps the question of Jesus' conception near the top of the agenda, but if people study this topic hoping for fresh light on Christian morality they are bound to be disappointed. To believe in the virginal conception of Jesus is not to believe that sex is bad; to disbelieve it because you believe that sex is a God-given gift is to miss the point. That is not what the question is about.

Conception and Scripture

A second preliminary point. Some Christians regard the debate about the virginal conception of Jesus as simply a test case for whether the Bible is completely 'true'. According to this view, if you hold a 'high' view of Scripture, you must accept that what Matthew and Luke wrote is true; if you deny the latter, you've gone soft on Scripture. This is sometimes coupled with the old debate about the meaning of Isaiah 7.14, the prophecy that 'a virgin shall conceive and bear a son'.

Numerous learned articles have been produced to show that the Hebrew word in question doesn't necessarily mean 'virgin' in our sense, and that Matthew simply misunderstood the passage. That conclusion has been waved around wildly by those who want to deny Jesus' virginal conception, but actually it is an irrelevant issue. The fact that Luke has a birth narrative, quite

different from Matthew's, in which also Jesus is described as
having been conceived without a human father, indicates (as
Spong recognizes from time to time) that the belief was quite
widespread in the early church. It wasn't a matter of Matthew
making it up on the basis of a misreading of Isaiah.

The larger question of Scripture itself is an important one,
but we can't go into it here, and anyway this, once more, isn't the
point. It is precisely because the Bible contains things like the
virginal conception of Jesus that some people, including some
devout Christians, have come to feel that the Bible cannot in
fact be as true as they had thought. One can't therefore simply
appeal to the truth of the Bible and hope that this will settle the
issue. It just begs the question. Fundamentalists, who are more
interested in the inerrancy of Scripture and the likelihood of
'miracles', will always miss the point in one direction;
'modernists' (Spong is definitely a 'modernist', not a 'post-
modernist'), who are more interested in saying what God cannot
do, will always miss the point in the other. The issue needs
addressing at another level altogether.

Science and Religion?

Another problem concerns the old debate between science and
religion. I have heard it seriously argued that we can no longer
believe in the virginal conception of Jesus now that we know all
that we do know, with the aid of modern medical research,
about the process of conception and birth. The ancients, we are
assured, didn't know about the scientific view of life, and so were
completely open to the possibility of all sorts of odd things happening here and there.

This again simply misses the point. We do, of course, have
access to all kinds of medical details that nobody in the first
century had dreamed of. Well, it is certainly true that we know a
good deal more than they did, at the level of *detail*. But the fact
remains that first-century folk knew every bit as well as we do
that babies are produced by sexual intercourse. When, in Matthew's version of the story, Joseph heard about Mary's preg-
nancy, his problem arose not because he didn't know the facts of
life, but because he did.

Virginal Conception and Incarnation

This brings us to what is perhaps a more central issue. Some muddled Christians have imagined that the virginal conception of Jesus was necessary, so to speak, for the incarnation to happen – in other words, for Jesus to be 'the Son of God'. If he had had two human parents in the ordinary way, it is felt, he would have been 'merely' human. With only one human parent, there was room for some other influence, namely, a divine parentage.

This is a nonsensical muddle. Orthodox Christianity has always insisted that Jesus is as totally human as any of us. If we claim that he is in some sense 'divine', that of itself has nothing to do with the supposition that he was conceived without a human father. The New Testament asserts *both* that Jesus was virginally conceived, *and* that Jesus is to be accorded divine honours by good Jewish-style monotheists. It does not make either of those beliefs dependent upon the other.

What about Luke 1.35? There we read that the angel said to Mary: 'The Holy Spirit will come upon you, and the power of the Most High will overshadow you; therefore the child to be born will be holy; he will be called Son of God.' Doesn't this indicate that Jesus' divinity was, at least for Luke, somehow connected to the virginal conception?

Not directly. 'Son of God' in the first century was first and foremost a title for Israel, and then for the true Messiah. It seems as though Paul took this title, which to begin with certainly didn't imply any doctrine of incarnation, and made it one of the focal points for his fresh understanding of Jesus. He clearly held the view that, as well as being a fully human being, Jesus was also, in some sense, on God's side of the equation as well. That is what seems to be going on in, for instance, Galatians 4.4, Romans 1.3–4, and Romans 8.3.

But 'Son of God' didn't get the full meaning that it now has within Christianity until much later. As for Luke, though he clearly shares Paul's belief in the incarnation, he keeps it very low-key throughout his gospel. This is not, fundamentally, what his birth narrative is all about. We may therefore safely say that, for the New Testament writers, the virginal conception of Jesus was not a way of asserting that he was, as it were, genetically divine on one side and genetically human on the other. That is a gross category mistake.

Supernatural?

There have been many Christians over the years, and there are
many today, for whom the point of Christianity is basically that it
is *supernatural*. It isn't so much that they believe in Jesus, and
then find that their worldview needs stretching to take in things
that they hadn't bargained for within their prevailing culture. It
is more that their basic commitment is to the idea of a supernatural dimension to life, and they find this conveniently confirmed by Jesus.

This supernaturalism has been under attack for the last two
hundred years. Frankly, it deserved it. It needs to be said as
clearly as possible that the 'supernatural' is not the same thing as
the 'Christian'. The great divide between the 'natural' and the
'supernatural', certainly in the way we use those words today,
comes basically from the eighteenth century, bringing with it the
whole debate about 'miracles'. Many Christians over the last two
centuries have thought that being Christian committed them to
believing in 'miracles', in the sense of irrational suspensions of
the normal laws of nature. Some have argued that miraculous
events are part of the evidence for the existence of God. Some
have even argued that Jesus' ability to perform miracles is part
of the evidence for his being the 'Son of God'. Sceptics have
turned the argument round: miracles don't occur, Jesus didn't do
any, therefore he wasn't 'the Son of God'.

This, as we saw, is one of the many claims that Barbara Thiering is making. We must, she says, give up a religion that is basically a form of supernaturalism. It is also what Rudolf Bultmann
was getting at when he said that we couldn't believe in miracles
now that we had modern medicine and the electric light. A. N.
Wilson continued in this same tradition. If it's 'supernatural',
then it didn't happen, because we know that 'supernatural'
things just don't happen: Q. E. D. Now Spong, predictably,
comes in on the same track.

I raise this here because the virginal conception is often used
as a sort of simple test case for whether you are prepared to
believe in 'miracles' or not. Again I stress: this is putting the cart
before the horse. The Greek New Testament doesn't actually
have a word that means 'miracle'; when things happened which
seemed to give normal ideas of reality some sort of jolt, the
gospel writers used words like 'signs', 'powerful acts', or

'paradoxes'. Believing in 'miracles', in the eighteenth-century sense, is no good as a test of genuine Christianity. On the one hand, plenty of people believe in 'miracles' without connecting them in any way with Jesus. On the other hand, the eighteenth-century idea of a 'miracle' envisaged a 'God' who was a remote, detached Being, who normally kept his hands clean from involvement with the space-time universe, but just occasionally used to 'intervene'. That is a total travesty of the biblical picture. If saying you believe in miracles commits you to that kind of picture of God, then it would be better for a Christian to refuse.

But what if the God who made the world has remained active within the world? What if the word 'God' itself might refer, not to this distant, remote, occasionally-intervening Being, but to a God who breathed with the breath of the world? What if this God, as the Old Testament says, feeds the young ravens when they call out, not (presumably) by dropping food 'miraculously' from the sky, but by being active *within* his creation, within 'instinct' and hidden motivations? When the Bible says that God commanded Adam and Eve to 'be fruitful and multiply', and gave them tasks to perform in relation to his creation, did this mean that he barked a command at them from a distance, or put up notices in Eden telling them what to do? Of course not. He put into their inmost beings, as creatures made to reflect his image into his world, a deep desire for one another, and a deep longing to create and nurture order and beauty within creation. This is a very different picture from the eighteenth-century one; it is much more Biblical, and at the same time (I think) much more believable. It puts the question of 'God' acting within the world into quite a different dimension.

New World, New Worldview

We have now cleared away some of the rubble that surrounds the issue of Jesus' conception. How, then, are we to move towards saying something positive about it?

We need to start at the proper place, namely, the resurrection. The central Christian claim is that Jesus of Nazareth was raised from the dead three days after his execution. I have argued in the previous chapter that as historians we are forced to take this claim very seriously indeed. The alternative explanations, when examined, turn out to be remarkably lame.

But, if this is so, we are forced to contemplate the possibility that there might after all be more things in heaven and earth than are dreamed of in our philosophies, whether of the eighteenth or the twentieth centuries. It is the resurrection, not the virginal conception, that breaks open all other worldviews and demands that the closed systems with which humans try to make sense of their world must be held open to allow for the God who, having created the world, has never for a moment abandoned it.

This does *not* mean that the resurrection throws open the door, after all, to a miscellaneous 'appeal to the supernatural'. I hold to what I said above. 'Natural' and 'supernatural', in the way those categories are regularly used today, are thoroughly misleading words. The resurrection throws open the door to a different belief, which looks like this. (1) The creator of the world, who never abandoned his world, called Israel to be the spearhead of his redeeming purposes for it. (2) This God has now, in Jesus, drawn together the threads of Israel's long destiny, in order to deal with evil in the world and to begin, dramatically, the creation of a new world. This new world is not superimposed upon the old one, but grows out of its very womb in a great act of new creation, like the oak from the acorn.

The resurrection thus challenges all views of the world, and of history, that insist on reducing everything to materialistic analysis. (It also challenges all views which reduce everything to pagan superstition or magic.) In this light, and in this light alone, we can approach the question of the conception of Jesus with some hope, not necessarily of understanding it, but of sketching out the area within which true understanding may perhaps be found. I stress, this is not an argument designed to convince sceptics on their own materialist ground. That is impossible. It is an argument which depends on the worldview created by, and around, the resurrection of Jesus – which, I have suggested, *is* something that has to be taken seriously by all historians of the first century.

Within the context of the resurrection, then, we may be able to see not only the possibility but also the meaning of Jesus' virginal conception. *If* God is who the Old Testament says he is; and *if* Jesus, believing what he did, went to his death to redeem

Israel and the world; and *if* he rose again from the dead; then the world of creation in general, and the history of Israel in par ticular, do not exist at a great distance from God, but are the very spheres of his loving, creative activity. What if, in the middle of Israel's history, we find that a man who claimed to embody her destiny had been raised from the dead after his execution? What if we find that, very early within the movement that grew up around him, there arose two independent sources claiming that he had been conceived without a human father? Faced with all this, a belief in this God, and this Jesus, may compel us to hold open the possibility that this account of his conception might just be true.

Compromise with Paganism?

Many arguments have been advanced by Christian apologists to back up this possibility. One in particular I find quite impressive. Both Matthew and Luke were taking an enormous risk. They must have known that they were opening the door to the possibility of deep misunderstanding. In the pagan world, stories of virginal conception were known, and were regularly open to the cynical reinterpretation that it was a cover-up for sexual misbehaviour. It is quite clear that both Matthew and Luke intended their stories to be taken seriously within the Jewish world that had so deeply informed their narratives, within which alone, in fact, they had their basic meaning. The natural tendency would have been to keep quiet. The fact that they spoke out, and took care to set their stories within an emphatically Jewish context, makes it clear that the early church – the very early church, not the second- or third-generation church as Spong suggests – was aware of something strange surrounding Jesus' birth, and that they were writing to clarify the matter.

This is important for the following reason. From early on in church history, some people have suggested that the Christians took a pagan idea (a divine figure with a miraculous birth) and projected it on to the Jewish Jesus, to whom (of course) such ideas would have been anathema. This suggestion, actually, cuts both ways. It is quite clear that early Christianity, certainly at the time of Matthew and Luke, was every bit as opposed to the sur- rounding paganism as early Judaism was. Why would Christians,

increasingly conscious of hostility from the pagan world, have
included a story like this, so likely to be misunderstood in a way
that they clearly could not intend? Not, certainly, to try to curry
favour. Neither Matthew nor Luke was writing to show pagan
audiences that Christianity was just like paganism! Why then
would they do it? One of the best possible answers is that they
very firmly believed it to be true. More than that, though: the
Christian claim always was that the Jewish story in general, and
the Christian climax to it in particular, was the truth, the reality,
of which paganism was the parody.

The trouble with a much-parodied truth is that, when the real
truth appears, it can easily be mistaken for just another parody.
But one cannot, for that reason alone, suppress the truth. And
Christianity claims that in the extraordinary conception of Jesus
we see the truth of which all those pagan stories are parodies. Of
course this is shocking. Of course it is an affront to other
worldviews. It only makes sense within the Judaeo-Christian
worldview, specifically within the worldview that is opened up by
the resurrection of Jesus.

The Gift of God

What possible meaning can this story have, if it isn't simply an
example of God 'suspending the laws of nature' (what sort of a
faith would *that* evoke?), or a 'proof' of Jesus' divinity, or a comment upon human sexuality? One clear option here, again in the
light of the entire Christian revelation, is to see, within the
apparent strangeness of the event, a sign of the total love and
grace of this God:

> Jesus is sheer, absolute gift of God. He is not a mere product
> of human history; he is the humanity of the God who gra-
> ciously identifies with us and shares our human condition. No
> less human for that, for God's solidarity with us requires his
> full humanity. But human *as* God's self-gift to humanity, as
> 'Immanuel'.[14]

Let us, then, at least be clear about the status of the question.
The virginal conception of Jesus is not, in itself, a central, major
doctrine of the New Testament. None of the epistle-writers men-

tions it at all; they, clearly, managed to mount their wide range of theological arguments without recourse to it. (It is sometimes said that Mark doesn't mention it, either; this is true, so far as it goes, but since Mark's gospel is quite possibly truncated at both ends it's impossible to tell what might have been there if we had the whole original book.) There are many Christians who have affirmed the doctrine for what seem to be very dubious reasons; sceptics, seeing this, have had every reason to continue in their scepticism. If Christians claim isolated oddities as of the essence of their faith, this seems an easy target.

But Christianity makes claims not just at the level of isolated occurrences, but at the level of worldviews. One of the central worldview claims of Christianity, based on the resurrection of Jesus seen in the context of the whole Jewish tradition, is that the creator God was active in and as Jesus to redeem Israel and the world. If that is true, then this is the truth for which all the world has longed, towards which all humanity has dimly been striving. And if that is so, in turn, then it is less surprising than it might otherwise have been to find the early Christians saying that Jesus' mother remained a virgin at the time of his conception. It is precisely the sort of strange truth which creeps up on you unawares, which takes you by surprise, but which then makes itself at home, fitting in unexpectedly well to the aspirations of Jew as well as of Greek. We cannot 'prove' the virginal conception of Jesus to the satisfaction of post-Enlightenment scepticism. But in the light of the resurrection we are called to be sceptical about scepticism itself.

Christmas: Fantasy and Reality

Spong, like A. N. Wilson, has no difficulty in showing that a good many of the traditional Christmas stories have no basis in the text. But that's not something that ought to worry any Christian. It is, actually, something that's routinely pointed out in sermons. We don't know (for instance) that there were *three* 'wise men'; that's a deduction we make from the fact that Matthew mentions three gifts. Nor is it likely that any visit from these 'Magi' coincided either in place or time with a visit from shepherds. The church has, of course, recognized this by separating the feasts of Christmas (the birth of Jesus) and Epiphany

(the visit of the 'wise men'); but in carol services and Christmas
cards alike the two are regularly muddled up in a grand jumble.

Argument by Caricature

So what? Christianity does not hinge in any way upon the pious
fantasies of devout people down the ages. It is based on history,
not fantasy. That is why it is disturbing, to return for a moment
to Wilson's treatment of the subject, to find his chapter on the
birth and childhood of Jesus such a strange mixture of serious
argument and irrelevant meandering.

One minute Wilson is all sober history, discussing Luke and
Josephus, Augustus and Quirinius. The next minute he is off
citing books which he admits were written two, three or four
hundred years later, which contain all sorts of wildly improbable
legends about Jesus' childhood, which nobody in their right mind
ever thought had any historical basis at all. He mixes all this up
with quotations from sentimental Victorian Christmas hymns,
and with his own experience: he was shown, as a tourist, the
grotto where Mary had sat down to suckle the baby Jesus on the
journey to Egypt, and he was offered chalk-dust from the walls
which, supposedly, had formed because of the drops of her
milk.[15] When, five pages later, we get the stories of Jesus visiting
Cornwall, it is hardly surprising that we find King Arthur as well.
The argument has degenerated into slapstick. 'You can't believe
all that rubbish,' Wilson seems to be saying, 'so of course you
can't believe any of the biblical stories either.' Actually, his argument backfires. When we read all the legends that did grow up
later about the birth and childhood of Jesus, one thing is very
striking. The gospels themselves, our earliest documents about
Jesus, are sober, restrained and understated by comparison.

Spong operates in a similar, though more restrained, way. It is
all very well to list angels, shepherds, an angry old king, wise
men, a star, and so forth, and to say that this is the stuff of which
legends are made. That doesn't prove anything at all. Everyone
agrees that legends were indeed made of them – in subsequent
Christian history. What we need to decide is *why* legends were
made of them. One strong possible reason is that there were
indeed some very strange goings-on at the time of Jesus' birth.
Let us take a couple of examples.

The King and the Star

The first example concerns the story that Herod the Great had all the young children in Bethlehem put to death (Matthew 2.16–18). Spong implies that this is incredible. But is it?

It is, frankly, incredible to me that someone living in the century of Hitler, Stalin and Pol Pot should find it difficult to believe that rulers can slaughter children for their own political ends. Furthermore, everything we know about Herod the Great (mostly from the Jewish historian Josephus, who had access to Herod's court records) suggests that he was exactly the sort of man who would have had all the babies in a particular village executed if he had had the slightest suspicion that anyone was talking about a future king being born there. After all, Josephus tells us that this same Herod, around the same time, had several of his own family murdered because of his paranoia about plots against his life. He also arranged for several leading citizens from around the country to be killed at the time of his own death, so that at least he would ensure that the nation would mourn for him in proper style, instead of celebrating as they might well otherwise have done.[16] It is no strain on the imagination to think that this same Herod would do what Matthew says he did.

Second, what about the wandering star? Spong knows, of course, that according to astronomical research there were two very remarkable phenomena in the years just before the birth of Jesus. Halley's Comet appeared around 12 BC; Jupiter, Saturn and Mars came together in an extremely rare collocation in 8 BC. Spong's comment on this (p. 92) is that 'When Christians, who stood on the other side of Easter, tried to imagine the moment when Jesus was born, both Halley's comet and the planetary juxtaposition could have been drawn into the interpretive framework.'

This, I suppose, is just about possible. We have, of course, no reason to think that the early Christians either had access to astronomical information, or even were interested in such things. Indeed, we have quite good reason to suppose that they would not have bothered their heads about such matters. But it is just about conceivable that they would (a) have heard about these phenomena independently of stories about Jesus, (b) have been able to calculate when they had happened, and (c) have then related them to the birth of Jesus. It's possible; but, speaking as a historian, I have to say that I do not think it is at all likely.

I do, however, think it really quite likely that, faced with remarkable astronomical occurrences, a few learned and devout pagans from countries beyond Judaea might take it into their heads that something extraordinary was afoot in the world of human affairs. Such people might quite easily, historically speaking, come looking for a king who, like Halley's Comet on that occasion, was to arise under the sign of the Lion (the comet was facing towards Leo; the Lion was of course the old symbol for the house of Judah).[17] None of this can be 'proved', of course, any more than any of Spong's, Wilson's or Thiering's assertions about 'what happened' can be 'proved'. History is not about that sort of absolute 'proof', but about weighing the balance of likelihood and unlikelihood.

A Great Census?

When historical sceptics like Wilson and Spong do run into a serious issue of historicity on which scholars can and do disagree, it is worth pointing out there are perfectly good options other than the ones they suggest. Wilson returns frequently to Luke's reference to the census which supposedly took place 'while Quirinius was governor of Syria' (Luke 2.2). The point is then (Wilson, p. 75; Spong, p. 142) that Quirinius, as we know from elsewhere, didn't become governor of Syria until about AD 6, getting on for ten years after the most likely date for Jesus' birth. Moral: Luke doesn't know what he is talking about. But is it really that simple?

A cautionary note before we address the topic itself. There is nothing to be gained from an attempt to make the truth of Christianity depend on the literal truth of every word of the Bible. Such a view shifts the balance in Christianity decisively in the wrong direction. For Christians, Jesus, not the New Testament, is the central truth. But one should not, for that reason, imagine that historical issues can simply go by the board. Just because we are not fundamentalists, that need not mean that we allow shoddy historical arguments to pass without comment.

The question of Quirinius and his census is an old chestnut, requiring a good knowledge of Greek. It depends on the meaning of the word *protos*, which usually means 'first'. Thus most translations of Luke 2.2 read 'this was the first [*protos*] census, when Quirinius was governor of Syria', or something like that. But in the Greek of the time, as the standard major Greek lexicons point out, the word *protos* came sometimes to be used to mean 'before', when followed (as this is) by the genitive case. A good example is in John 1.15, where John the Baptist says of Jesus 'he was *before me*', with the Greek being again *protos* followed by the genitive of 'me'.[18] I suggest, therefore, that actually the most natural reading of the verse is: 'This census took place *before the time when* Quirinius was governor of Syria.'[19]

This solves an otherwise odd problem: why should Luke say that Quirinius' census was the *first*? Which later ones was he thinking of? This reading, of course, does not resolve all the difficulties. We don't know, from other sources, of a census earlier than Quirinius'. But there are a great many things that we don't know in ancient history. There are huge gaps in our records all over the place. Only those who imagine that one can study history by looking up back copies of the London *Times* or the *Washington Post* in a convenient library can make the mistake of arguing from silence in matters relating to the first century.

My guess is that Luke knew a tradition in which Jesus was born during some sort of census, and that Luke knew as well as we do that it couldn't have been the one conducted under Quirinius, because by then Jesus was about ten years old. That is why he wrote that the census was the one *before* that conducted by Quirinius. Whatever we conclude, there is on this matter, and on a good many others, much more to be said than Wilson and Spong allow for.

Back to Fantasy

There is plenty in Spong's book which appears plausible enough. On several issues, what he says is unexceptional in terms of the run of contemporary New Testament scholarship. In addition, some of his protests against the subjugation of women within the church have some validity, even if he does become a little hysterical in linking the problem so directly to Matthew's and

Luke's birth stories, and even if he does give an amazingly caricatured picture of church history in order to sustain his rhetoric.[20] But in the concluding chapters of his work he gives rein to pure fantasy, which in the event puts him well outside the bracket of serious scholarship, or even serious scepticism of the A. N. Wilson variety.

His final contentions are worthy of Barbara Thiering. He argues, first, that Jesus was conceived illegitimately, and quite probably by an act of sexual violence, i.e. rape. Ironically, a good deal of his 'argument' here consists of very literalistic readings of a few passages in the gospels, like the wedding at Cana (see below). Like Thiering's 'pesher', his 'midrash' is quickly abandoned when necessary. Most of his suggestions in this area are, he admits, highly speculative. It is mainly an appeal to a radical Christian imagination: if we can find God in a human figure bruised, beaten and dying on a cross, can we not also find him in one conceived in an act of violence? Put like that, the answer is, of course, yes; but there are many guises in which one *could* 'find God' and yet which nobody supposes were true of the real Jesus.

He finally suggests that Jesus was married, quite probably to Mary Magdalene. One of his most ingenious arguments (p. 192) is that Jesus and his mother attended a wedding together, in Cana of Galilee (John 2.1–11). At this point the level of his argument needs to be seen to be believed:

> When two generations are present at a wedding it is almost always a family affair. I have never attended a wedding with my mother except when it was the wedding of a relative. The only time my mother and my closest friends were at a wedding together with me was my own wedding!
>
> So John tells us that at this wedding Jesus, Jesus' disciples, and Jesus' mother were all in attendance. Whose wedding was it? The narrative does not say, but the narrative does say that the mother of Jesus was quite concerned that the wine supply was exhausted . . . do guests at a wedding become upset about such details? No, but the mother of the bridegroom . . . certainly would be upset . . .

This is where the chickens come home to roost. Having set up a scheme of pseudo-'midrash' in which, as Spong himself admits, 'the imagination is free to roam and speculate', then all things are indeed possible – though, again, it is ironic that Spong chooses to treat the narrative of John 2, which is as pregnant with symbolism as anything else in the New Testament, as straight reportage, not as 'midrash'.

Spong argues from his own experience about who goes to which weddings. But Spong has not thought what it was like to live in peasant society in first-century Galilee. There, in a small community, a wedding was a whole-village affair, and quite probably a several-villages affair. Nazareth and Cana were close neighbours. It is highly likely that whole families in one village would go to a whole-family wedding in the next one. Not to see this is to betray a total lack of historical perspective. Upon such slender and anachronistic threads hang Spong's entire argument.

Spong has, in short, cut himself off from serious historical study. The world that he has opened up is a world which he himself calls midrash, however inaccurately. It is a world where the modern exegete can reconstruct a fantasy-history in the interests of a current ideology, in Spong's case a resolute insistence upon bringing issues of sexuality into everything. At last we see the nature of his whole argument. Having insisted that Matthew and Luke wrote 'midrash', inventing stories which didn't happen in order to reflect their own ideologies, Spong is now tacitly claiming to stand in the same tradition, writing fiction upon which to base his own contemporary agendas. This may be ingenious, but it is neither serious history nor serious theology.

This is a pity. We desperately need, in the contemporary church, to think seriously through the historical and theological issues of the origins of Christianity, on the one hand, and the nature of sexuality, on the other. But we will never succeed in either of these tasks if we take Spong as a guide. He lashes out wildly at those who still embrace that fundamentalism from which he himself has escaped, and succeeds in knocking all the china off the shelf in the process. He claims the status of persecuted hero (p. 175), along with John Robinson, David Jenkins, and Hans Küng, though he lacks the deep historical sense of the first, the quicksilver mind of the second, and the enormous learning of the third.

Spong's summons to follow where he leads cannot be dismissed merely as the blind leading the blind. He sees some things – but sees them through a tiny peephole and in a glaring bright light. Dazzled, he rushes on, constructing imaginary historical worlds and inviting us to base our faith and life upon them. If we refuse this invitation he will, no doubt, hurl his favourite abuse-word at us again. But if everyone who disagrees with Spong's book turns out to be a fundamentalist, then I suppose that all the fundamentalist churches in the world would not be able to contain the new members who would suddenly arrive on their doorsteps.

5

Jesus Revisited

Back to the Portrait Gallery

We have returned to the portrait gallery, only to find that it has had three caricatures added to its collection. They have each grasped one or two features of a true portrait, but the results are misshapen and distorted. We have done our best, like Schweitzer, to pull them off the walls. What can we, in our turn, put up in their place?

There are siren voices around which tell us that it would be better not to try. Don't even attempt to reconstruct Jesus: be content to know that his ethos remains in the room where the portraits used to hang, that his memory is alive in the circle of those who meet there. C. S. Lewis, a widely respected figure in conservative Christian circles, counselled against trying to rediscover Jesus by historical means. In his best-selling book *The Screwtape Letters*, he made out that the quest for Jesus was really the work of the devil . . . and that any right-minded Christian should back off from it. This, frankly, is odd; in his own professional sphere, that of English literature, Lewis did more than most to help people understand old writings in their proper historical context. Why should he not want them to do the same with Jesus?

Because, presumably, he didn't like the portraits that had been produced to date. And who can blame him? No doubt there are many devout people who, faced with Thiering, Wilson and Spong, will have exactly the same reaction.

But the task remains vital. It's been said often enough, but it bears repeating: without the real human Jesus of Nazareth, we are at the mercy of anybody who tells us that 'Christ' is this, or that. Even Spong, claiming to go back to history, insists as we saw on 'my Christ'. So where do we start?

Jesus Within Judaism

We begin, as Schweitzer rightly insisted, with Jesus' Jewish context. What did it mean to be a first-century Palestinian Jew?

It meant, first, a setting of *social unrest*. Josephus tells us of several incidents in the time of Jesus in which Roman soldiers acted violently towards the populace; no doubt there were plenty of localized incidents of which we know nothing. Taxation was high, breeding frustration and resentment. Tensions within the Jewish community – poor against rich, different religious pressure groups arguing their case – were just as fierce in some instances as anger against Rome. Popular movements sprang up like plants in shallow soil, withered quickly in the heat of Roman repression, and ended (usually) with the death or disappearance of the leaders, and the dispersal of the disillusioned followers.

Second, therefore, it meant a setting of *mounting expectation*. Israel had returned from exile in Babylon several hundred years earlier, but she was still not free. The *real* 'return from exile' would surely come soon. Some Jews studied the ancient prophecies for signs, and tried to calculate the chronological moment when God would act. Others grew tired of waiting for God, and decided to take matters into their own hands. Others decided that the best thing to do was to intensify their observance of the traditional laws. Some hoped, in a fairly ill-defined way, that God would send a great King who, as Messiah, would lead them in victory over their enemies. All of these expectations were regularly expressed in highly charged language, including that which we call 'apocalyptic' – stars falling from heaven, and so forth. This, as we saw, didn't mean that they thought the physical world would end. Rather, they looked for an end to the present way the world was running, and for a great turn-around in which they would come out on top.

Third, this hope was *enacted* by all sorts of festivals, liturgies, and readings from sacred books. Pilgrimage to Jerusalem at Passover time, in particular, was a dramatic celebration and re-enactment of God's deliverance of his people from their old foes, and hence a constant reminder that he would do so again. God would become King! No more Romans, no more Herod, no more corrupt chief priests ... simply God, a Messiah, and an Israel devout, holy, and above all free.

Those who thronged the holy city at these times were celebrating basic Jewish theology, not as a set of abstract intellectual ideas, but as the reality which gave meaning to their puzzling lives. There was one God, the creator of all, and this God had chosen Israel to be his special people. Soon he would show his covenant-faithfulness by rescuing Israel from her enemies, these great mythical monsters who came from the sea to attack her in the guise of pagan armies. Israel would be like Daniel rescued from the lion's den, the human figure snatched up from among the wild beasts. And when this happened ... it could mean nothing short of cosmic renewal. God's exaltation of Israel would be the moment when the whole chaotic world would be brought back into order. Therefore, many believed, God would raise from the dead at that time all the great saints of old. All Israel, past and present, would be physically raised to a new life. The nation, and the world, would be reborn.

It was to this people that Jesus came. It was these whispers that he heard in the lanes and backyards of his native Galilee. It was these aspirations that he found himself called to fulfil. But his method of fulfilling them was the most paradoxical thing in Israel's long and puzzling history.

Jesus Within the Gospels

Before we can look at Jesus' own agenda, we must say two more words about the gospels, which we have already discussed in previous chapters. The way to find the real Jesus is, as it were, by a pincer movement: forwards from the picture of first-century Judaism; backwards from the gospels.

This, as we have seen, has often been declared impossible. The gospels (we are told) are faith-documents: therefore, they are not about history. The gospels are the product of long theological reflection: therefore, they are not biographies. The first thing to be said to this is that these are false alternatives. Of course the gospels are written from a point of view; so is all history. Christian faith is no more necessarily misleading as a point of view than modern agnosticism or atheism. Would you trust a book on Beethoven written by someone who was tone-deaf? As we have seen, the gospels do conform to the first-century standard of what biographies looked like – including their long

sections on the death of the subject, which was by no means
unknown as a feature of ancient biography. This does not mean
that they are not theologically reflective works; only that they
are theologically reflective *biographies*.

The second thing that must be said is that the theological
reflection which they offer is emphatically Jewish. Like Jesus
himself, they wear their Jewish ancestry on page after page. And
the great thing about first-century Judaism, from this point of
view, was its concentration on history. If you tried to tell an
average first-century Jew that God had redeemed his people,
and invited him to believe this despite the fact that Israel was
still under Roman rule, that the ancestral law was not being
obeyed by most Jews, that the world as a whole was still full of
arrogance and evil – he would say that you had simply not
understood what you were talking about. What mattered at the
end of the day was *history*. Something had to happen in the real
world. This is why, as historians, we have to grapple with the
question which we raised in chapter 3: what, *historically*, had
occurred shortly after Jesus' death, to make first-century Jews
say that the great redemption had indeed happened? A
'spiritual' redemption that left historical reality unaffected was a
contradiction in terms. If the gospels, seen in terms of the pagan
culture to which the church went in mission, are inescapably
biographies, then, seen in terms of the Jewish culture which gave
them their theological depth, they are inescapably *theological
history*.

This doesn't mean, of course, that they put everything in
chronological order, or reported everything Jesus (or anyone
else) said in exactly the words that he used. No historian ever
does that. New Testament scholars who worry about the obvious
fact that the gospels put incidents in different orders are simply
being naive. When Churchill's biographer, Martin Gilbert,
brought out a one-volume version of his multi-volume *magnum
opus*, one reviewer criticized it quite sharply for being a mere
chronological list of events. That's not what real history looks
like.

But it does mean that the gospels must be taken seriously as
historical, as well as theological and faith-based, documents. We
are not committing a gross error in looking to them for serious
information about the Jesus who lived within first-century
Judaism. Of course we must learn to understand the special

language-systems they use. We have seen that Thiering's 'pesher' method, and Spong's 'midrash' theory, are based on thin air. But there are other guidelines.

We mustn't imagine that the parables of Jesus describe actual events. We mustn't imagine that 'apocalyptic' language is to be read in a flat, literal manner. We mustn't imagine that the short 'anecdotes' which occupy most of Mark's gospel, and a good bit of Matthew and Luke, happened exactly as described: most of them would have been over in about one minute, leaving the impression of Jesus undertaking a breathless whistle-stop tour around the Galilean villages. We must, in other words, understand the literary form and genre of the different bits of writing. Brief and clipped anecdotes have obviously been shaped by constant retelling within the church. Apocalyptic writing invests space-time reality with theological significance. Parables are stories designed to break open worldviews and make new understanding possible. If we keep our literary wits about us, there is no reason why we should not be able to make a fair start at understanding the Jesus of the gospels as the Jesus of first-century Palestine.

Jesus and the Kingdom of God

'No King but God' was the revolutionary slogan of the day. If you had been a Galilean peasant, working in your smallholding, your impression of Jesus would have been that he was a prophet who was announcing that God was now at last becoming King. This could only mean one thing: Israel was at last going to be redeemed, rescued from oppression. God's 'Kingdom' wasn't a state of mind, or a sense of inward peace. It was concrete, historical, real.

Twentieth-century Western Christians need to shed a few ideas at this point. When people downed tools for a while and trudged off up a hillside to hear this Jesus talking, we can be sure they weren't going to hear someone tell them to be nice to each other; or that if they behaved themselves (or got their minds round the right theological scheme) there would be a rosy future waiting for them when they got to 'heaven'; or that God had decided at last to do something about forgiving them for their sins. First-century Jews knew that they ought to be nice to each other. In so far as they thought at all about life after death, they believed that their God would look after them, and eventually give them new physical bodies in his renewed world. (The phrase 'Kingdom of Heaven', which we find in Matthew's gospel, does *not* mean 'a Kingdom-place called "heaven".' It is a reverent way of saying 'the King*ship* of God'.) There is no sign that first-century Jews were walking around gloomily wondering how their sins were ever going to be forgiven. They had the Temple and the sacrificial system, which took care of all that. If Jesus had only said what a lot of Western Christians seem to think he said, he would have been just a big yawn-maker.

What he in fact said was so revolutionary that it woke everybody up. It was so dramatic that Jesus seems to have adopted a deliberate policy of keeping to the villages, always moving quickly on, never getting into the big Galilean towns like Sepphoris, just over the hill from Nazareth, or Tiberias, down by the sea of Galilee, just south of Magdala. Why? What was so different?

Double Revolution

The strange thing about Jesus' announcement of the Kingdom of God was that he managed *both* to claim that he was fulfilling the old prophecies, the old hopes, of Israel *and* to do so in a way which radically subverted them. The Kingdom of God is here, he seemed to be saying, *but it's not like you thought it was going to be.*

How so? When Israel's God acts, the Gentiles will benefit as well! When Israel's God brings in his new world, some of Israel's cherished traditions (like the food laws) will be swept away, no longer needed in the new worldwide family! Abraham, Isaac and Jacob will sit down in the Kingdom and welcome people from all over the world, while some of the sons of the Kingdom will be cast out. It's no wonder Jesus needed to use parables to say all this. If too many people realized the doubly revolutionary implications, he wouldn't have lasted five minutes.

Doubly revolutionary: first, anyone saying that Israel's God was becoming King was raising a standard for revolution, and, as Jesus himself wryly noted, all and sundry, particularly those bent on violence, would try to get in on the act. Second, to claim to be

announcing the Kingdom while at the same time subverting
Israel's national institutions, and/or the fiercely held agendas of
certain pressure groups, was asking for trouble. It would be like
announcing in a Moslem country that one was fulfilling the will
of Allah – while apparently vilifying Muhammad and burning a
copy of the Koran.

The Great Celebration

In particular, Jesus' characteristic behaviour spoke as many
volumes as his characteristic teaching. Wherever he went, there
was a party. After all, if God is becoming King at last, who
wouldn't want to celebrate? But he celebrated *with all the wrong
people*. He went into low dives and back alleys. He knocked
back the wine with the shady and disrespectable. He allowed
women of the street to come and fawn over him. And all the
time he seemed to be indicating that, as far as he was concerned,
they were in the process being welcomed into the new day that
was dawning, the day of God's becoming King. That was the significance of his remarkable healings (which, incidentally, most
serious scholars today are prepared to admit as historical).

What had happened to all the old taboos, to Israel's standards
of holiness? They seemed to have gone by the board. Jesus was
saying – in his actions as much as in his words – that you didn't
have to observe every last bit of the Torah before you would
count as a real member of Israel. He was saying that you didn't
have to make the journey to Jerusalem, offer sacrifice, and go
through purity rituals, in order to be regarded as clean, forgiven,
restored as a member of Israel. You could be healed, restored,
and forgiven right here, where Jesus was, at this party, just by
being there with him and welcoming his way of bringing in the
Kingdom. No wonder his family said he was out of his mind.

Not only his family. The pressure groups that were urging
Israel to become more holy, more faithful to Torah, would be
furious. This man was undermining everything they were trying
to do. The revolutionaries would be puzzled, then angry. This
man was using their language but meaning the wrong thing by it;
every serious radical politician knew that you had to organize,
sharpen up the weapons, and be ready to fight. And even Jesus'
closest followers, who at a certain point came to the conclusion

that Jesus was indeed the Messiah, not just a great prophet, seem to have remained puzzled by what he was actually trying to achieve.

Well, what *was* he trying to achieve? At this point we are back with Albert Schweitzer's set of questions. What did Jesus expect to happen? Was he disappointed?

The Aims of Jesus

We can safely say that Jesus didn't expect the world to come to an end. That bizarre idea, which has been touted around the learned halls of New Testament scholarship all this century, should now be given a pauper's funeral. Schweitzer was 100% right to say that Jesus should be understood in terms of Jewish apocalyptic. He was 100% wrong in saying what that language meant.

The Coming Crisis

As we have seen, this 'apocalyptic' language meant that Israel was on the verge of the great turn-around of the ages. The long night of exile was coming to an end; the great day of liberation was dawning. Israel was like a bride on the eve of her wedding day, or a prisoner on the verge of release after a mammoth sentence. Everything, everything is going to be different from now on. The world will be a different place. The birds will sound as though they're singing a different song. That's how apocalyptic language works. It invests ordinary events with their total significance. The monsters will be destroyed; the man will be exalted. 'The Son of Man will come on the clouds with power and great glory.' Israel will be vindicated, and her oppressors will trouble her no more.

Jesus picked up this massive expectation – *and applied it to himself.* He had welcomed sinners and outcasts into the Kingdom, calmly and quietly implying that this Kingdom was being redefined around himself. (Is it necessary to say at this point that this *doesn't* mean that he was an egotist, or that he imagined himself to be playing at being 'God' in some high-and-mighty sense?) As many prophets and other leaders had said in olden times (we may think of Elijah, or Isaiah, or John the Baptist), Israel's God was redefining his people, and was now doing so in and through the work of this one man. But what Jesus grasped, which so many of his contemporaries, like so many modern readers, failed to pick up was that Israel's destiny was now moving swiftly towards its vital, crucial moment. Israel, the historical people of the one creator God, was swimming in the stream of history just above a roaring waterfall. If she didn't watch out, she would be swept right over, and fall to her doom.

It didn't take much insight for Jesus to make that last point. Anyone with open eyes and ears could see that the Romans would only take so much provocation, and would then come and smash Jerusalem, and the nation, into little bits. Where Jesus' prophetic insight came into play was in the awesome realization that *when this happened, it would be the judgment of Israel's God on his wayward people.* Israel was called to be the light of the world, but the light was turned inwards on to itself. Israel was called to be the peacemaker, but she was bent on violent revolution. Israel was called to be the healer, but she was determined to dash the pagans to pieces like a potter's vessel. Jesus saw the judgment coming, and realized that it was not just from Rome, but from God. His first aim, therefore, was to summon Israel to 'repent' – not so much of petty individual sins, but of the great national rebellion, against the creator, the covenant God. Failure to repent would lead her inexorably towards disaster.

Jesus and Israel

His second aim, though, was the one that still sends shivers down the spine two thousand years later. As Schweitzer saw in one of his greatest insights, Jesus believed himself called to go out ahead of Israel, to meet the judgment in her place, alone. He drew on the old Jewish beliefs of the coming great tribulation, the time of bitter and harsh suffering and testing for the people of God. This 'tribulation' would surely come; but if he went out to meet it, to take it upon himself, then he might bear it on behalf of his people, so that they would not need to bear it. He would make a way through the tribulation, through the darkest night of Israel's exile and distress, and out the other side into the glorious light of the new day that would then dawn.

This, I believe, is far and away the best historical explanation
for Jesus' attitude in facing his own death. It is fascinating that
at this point A. N. Wilson seems to agree (p. 178f.):

> Jesus predicts that the Son of Man will die for his people as a
> ransom, and rise again ... [It is] quite possible that he did
> make such predictions about himself. He used metaphors
> such as drinking of a bitter cup, preparing himself for a bap-
> tism, and completing a great work, when he spoke of this final
> consummation ...
>
> It would not be impossible ... to suppose that Jesus
> foresaw his death, and in a way wished for it. He had by now
> come to see himself as a 'king', a man who could unify Israel
> and inaugurate the new 'kingdom of the saints'. ... By his
> prophetic witness, begun in Galilee and completed in
> Jerusalem, he thought that he would inaugurate the new age.
> When he had died, he would rise again; by implication, not
> only would he rise again, but so would the rest of the
> redeemed Israel. The rule of the saints would begin. Jesus,
> riding into the city on a donkey, believed that some such
> process was about to start.

This, I think, is almost exactly right. The Jewish hope was that
when Israel's strange destiny reached its fulfilment, the world
would be saved. Jesus' variation on that theme was his belief
that it would all happen through his own life, death and resurrection. Though scholars have often professed to doubt whether
Jesus could have predicted his own resurrection, even a cursory
study of Jewish literature of the period will set things straight.
Anyone who had read the books of the Maccabees would know
that those who die as martyrs for God's cause will be raised
again, physically, bodily. If the Maccabean martyrs could think
that, then so could Jesus.

If Wilson can accept all this, as it seems he can, what then
stops him from seeing that it might have actually happened?
Why is it so improbable that a Jesus who could think like this
should plan for his followers to become, after his death, the
spearheads of this renewed Israel, going into all the world with
the news that the God of Israel is after all the creator God, the
loving, redeeming God, of all the world? Why (in other words)

should a Jesus like this not plan for a community of his followers to continue his work?

What is so difficult, either, about the suggestion that this Jesus should give his followers, on the night he was betrayed, a symbol which would sum up in a simple action his whole drawing on to himself of Israel's national destiny? Why should he not bequeath to them a Passover-meal-with-a-difference, in which they would strangely know his presence, and be sustained by him, as they went about the task of implementing his decisive achievement?

What, ultimately, is so problematic about the suggestion that someone who could think these thoughts about himself and his vocation would thereby understand himself to be doing in person what, according to the Old Testament, Israel's God alone can do – namely, rescuing his people from their plight? Why should such a person, a good first-century Jewish monotheist, not also come to hold the strange and risky belief that the one true God, the God of Israel, was somehow present and active in him and even *as* him?

And what, we may ask, is so difficult about accepting for oneself that this claim of Jesus might be true? Aye, there's the rub: to do this will cost not less than everything. But that is perhaps what one should expect. Pearls of great price do not come cheap.

Notes

Chapter One. The Portraits and the Puzzles

1. e.g. Stephen Neill and Tom Wright, *The Interpretation of the New Testament, 1861–1986* (new edn.; Oxford: OUP, 1988), esp. chs. 4, 6 and 9; *Anchor Bible Dictionary* (New York: Doubleday, 1992), vol. 3, pp. 796–802.
2. *The Quest of the Historical Jesus* (Eng. Trans.; London: A. & C. Black, 1954), p. 396.
3. See the discussion in Karl Barth, *Protestant Theology in the Nineteenth Century* (Eng. Trans.; London: SCM, 1972), pp. 234–65.
4. cf. William Wrede, *The Messianic Secret* (London and Cambridge: James Clarke, 1971; German original, 1901).
5. London: Hodder & Stoughton, 1960; German original, 1956.
6. London: Collins, 1979; Dutch original, 1974.
7. London: SCM, 1971; German original also 1971.
8. e.g. *The Parables of the Kingdom* (London: Nisbet, 1935 and subsequent editions).
9. B. H. Mack, *A Myth of Innocence: Mark and Christian Origins* (Philadelphia: Fortress Press, 1988).
10. J. D. Crossan, *The Historical Jesus: The Life of a Mediterranean Jewish Peasant* (San Francisco and Edinburgh: HarperSanFrancisco and T. & T. Clark, 1991).
11. 'Gnostic' refers to a set of beliefs held by some on the fringes of the second- and third-century church. Crossan's position is also taken by writers like Elaine Pagels, *The Gnostic Gospels* (London: Penguin, 1980). It is fair to say that the vast majority of New Testament scholars would disagree.
12. S. G. F. Brandon, *Jesus and the Zealots* (Manchester: Manchester University Press, 1967); G. Vermes, *Jesus the Jew* (London: Collins, 1973).
13. cf. E. Bammel and C. F. D. Moule, *Jesus and the Politics of his Day* (Cambridge: CUP 1984).
14. Meyer, *The Aims of Jesus* (London: SCM, 1979); and also 'Jesus Christ', in *Anchor Bible Dictionary* vol. 3, pp. 773–96. Harvey, *Jesus and the Constraints of History* (London: Duckworth, 1982). Borg, *Conflict, Holiness and Politics in the Teachings of Jesus* (New York and Toronto: Edwin Mellen Press, 1984); compare also Borg, *Jesus: A New Vision* (San Francisco: Harper & Row, 1987) – this is a more popular and accessible version. Sanders, *Jesus and Judaism* (London: SCM, 1985).
15. It is extraordinary to me that Crossan's large work should make only fleeting mention of Borg and Sanders, and not even acknowledge the

existence of Meyer and Harvey. The same is largely true of the probing and challenging book of John Bowden, *Jesus: the Unanswered Questions* (London: SCM, 1988). If Bowden had, for instance, brought Ben Meyer's work into his discussion, several of his questions would have looked very different, and perhaps more answerable.

Chapter Two. Barbara Thiering: Jesus in Code

1. cf. e.g. M. Baigent and R. Leigh, *The Dead Sea Scrolls Deception* (London: Cape, 1991).
2. All of which are published, in the series 'Australia and New Zealand Studies in Theology and Religion', by Theological Explorations, Sydney.
3. For a balanced assessment, see Geza Vermes, *The Dead Sea Scrolls: Qumran in Perspective* (London: Collins, 1977), pp. 142–56.
4. Habakkuk Commentary, column 9 lines 8–10. I take the translation from G. Vermes, *The Dead Sea Scrolls in English*, 3rd edn. (London: Pelican, 1987), p. 240.
5. Saturday, 26 September 1992, p. 16.
6. Matthew 26.6.
7. W. W. Isenberg, in J. M. Robinson (ed.), *The Nag Hammadi Library in English* (Leiden: E. J. Brill, 1977), p. 131.
8. Robinson, op. cit., p. 138. The other quotations are from the same page and p. 139.
9. Scholarly discussions of the passage may be found in Philip R. Davies, *The Damascus Covenant* (Sheffield: JSOT Press, 1982), pp. 113–16; Michael A. Knibb, *The Qumran Community* (Cambridge: CUP, 1987), pp. 42f. The passage seems to include criticism not just of those who take a second wife, but of polygamists.
10. On this, and other details about crucifixion in the ancient world, see M. Hengel, *Crucifixion* (London: SCM, 1977).
11. Dolores Cannon, *Jesus and the Essenes: Fresh Insights into Christ's Ministry and the Dead Sea Scrolls* (Bath: Gateway Books, 1992).

Chapter Three. A. N. Wilson: A Moderately Pale Galilean

1. A. N. Wilson, *Against Religion* (London: Chatto & Windus, 1991).
2. A. N. Wilson, *Jesus* (London: Sinclair-Stevenson, 1992). Page references in the rest of this chapter are to this book unless otherwise indicated.
3. On Vermes, see above, p. 13f.
4. cf. E. P. Sanders, *Paul and Palestinian Judaism: A Comparison of Patterns of Religion* (London: SCM, 1977). At a more accessible level, see Sanders, *Paul* (Past Masters; Oxford: OUP, 1991).
5. Wilmington, Del.: Michael Glazier/Notre Dame University Press, 1980.
6. The page-reference Wilson gives to a work by the German scholar Jeremias does not help much, since Wilson refers to an old, much shorter edition of the book than the one scholars now use.
7. See particularly *NTPG* ch. 9.

8. What follows is dependent on *NTPG*, pp. 248–59. See too E. P. Sanders, *Judaism: Practice and Belief, 63 BCE—66 CE* (London and Philadelphia: SCM and TPI, 1992), pp. 242–7. On Paul's reworking of monotheism, putting Jesus actually inside it, see my book *The Climax of the Covenant*, chs. 4, 5 and 6.
9. On Jesus as 'Word', see John 1.1–14; as 'Wisdom', see Colossians 1.15–20, which, like John 1, is heavily dependent upon the Jewish Wisdom tradition; as 'Torah', e.g. Galatians 6.2 and elsewhere; as 'Shekinah', John 1.14, and cf. below.
10. On this whole theme, see now especially John V. Taylor, *The Christlike God* (London: SCM, 1992).
11. *Reading the Old Testament: Method in Biblical Study* (London: Darton, Longman & Todd, 1984), p. 17.
12. 'The Church's One Foundation', by S. J. Stone (1839–1900).
13. On James, and on the rest of Jesus' family within the early church, see especially Richard J. Bauckham, *Jude and the Relatives of Jesus* (Edinburgh: T. & T. Clark, 1990).
14. Schillebeeckx, op. cit., pp. 379–97.

Chapter 4. John Spong: The Bishop and the Birth

1. HarperSanFrancisco, 1992. Page references in this chapter are to this book unless otherwise noted.
2. Garden City, New York: Doubleday, 1977. Compare also the supplements to this in *Catholic Biblical Quarterly* 48, 1986, pp. 468–83, 660–80.
3. cf. p. 8.
4. cf. E. Gellner, *Postmodernism, Reason and Religion* (London and New York: Routledge, 1992).
5. cf. *NTPG* chs. 13–14.
6. cf. G. Vermes, *Post-Biblical Jewish Studies* (Leiden: E. J. Brill, 1975); J. Neusner, *Midrash in Context: Essays in Formative Judaism* (Atlanta: Scholars' Press, 1988).
7. cf. H. L. Strack and G. Stemberger, *Introduction to the Talmud and Midrash* (Edinburgh: T. & T. Clark, 1991); P. S. Alexander, 'Midrash and the Gospels', in C. M. Tuckett (ed.), *Synoptic Studies* (Sheffield: JSOT Press, 1984), pp. 1–18, and 'Midrash', in R. J. Coggins and J. L. Houlden (eds.), *A Dictionary of Biblical Interpretation* (London and Philadelphia: SCM and TPI, 1990), pp. 452–9. Cf. too G. G. Portón, 'Midrash', in *Anchor Bible Dictionary*, vol. IV, pp. 818–22, with extensive bibliography.
8. Alexander 1984, p. 10, in direct reference to the question of Luke 1–2.
9. Alexander 1984, p. 12–15.
10. cf. *NTPG* Part III, esp. ch. 8.
11. Alexander 1984, p. 12.
12. Richard A. Burridge, *What are the Gospels? A Comparison with Graeco-Roman Biography* (Cambridge: CUP 1992).
13. There is a very good, full discussion of the relevant issues in C. E. B. Cranfield, 'Some Reflections on the Subject of the Virgin Birth', in *Scottish Journal of Theology* 41, 1988, pp. 177–89.

14. R. Bauckham and R. D. Williams, 'Jesus – God With Us', in C. Baxter (ed.), *Stepping Stones* (London: Hodder & Stoughton, 1987), p. 39.
15. Wilson, p. 82.
16. Josephus *Antiquities* 17.174–9.
17. See the cautious discussion in R. Brown, *The Birth of the Messiah*, pp. 170–3.
18. The phrase is repeated in John 1.30; compare also 15.18, where Jesus says 'the world hated me *before* [it hated] *you*', where again the Greek is *protos* with the genitive. Other references, in biblical and non-biblical literature of the period, may be found in the Greek Lexicon of Liddell and Scott (Oxford: OUP, 1940), p. 1535, and the *Greek-English Lexicon of the New Testament* of W. Bauer, revised and edited by Arndt, Gingrich and Danker (Chicago: Chicago University Press), p. 725f.
19. This solution has been advanced by various scholars, including, interestingly, William Temple in his *Readings in St John's Gospel* (London: Macmillan, 1945), p. 17; cf. most recently John Nolland, *Luke 1—9:20* (Dallas: Word Books, 1989), p. 101f. As to a related matter: Mary wouldn't have been required to go with Joseph, since wives were not taxed separately; but if she was indeed about to give birth, it is surely perfectly historically credible that Joseph should take her with him rather than leaving her alone.
20. See particularly pp. 201–21. Spong offers no evidence whatever for his repeated claim (e.g. pp. 198, 207) that negative attitudes towards women came into the Christian story in the early years of the second century. The much later ramblings of some off-beam theologians who speculated about whether Mary could have remained a virgin during the birth process, invoking (for instance) the way in which the risen Jesus passed through locked doors (p. 214f.), are of no more relevance to the real issues than the ramblings of off-beam theologians in our own day.